HOW TO SELECT

EMBROIDERED ART

Rhys Wesley & Ren Yue Yuan

mc Marshall Cavendish
名创国际出版集团

五洲传播出版社

图书在版编目（CIP）数据

如何挑选中国刺绣：英文／（澳大利亚）卫瑞斯，任月圆著.
－北京：五洲传播出版社，2009.1
ISBN·978－7－5085－1483－3

Ⅰ．如… Ⅱ．①卫…②任… Ⅲ．刺绣－简介－中国－英文 Ⅳ.J523.6

中国版本图书馆CIP数据核字（2008）第182829号

著　者：Rhys Wesley（澳大利亚）任月圆
选题编辑：张丽平 荆孝敏
责任编辑：张美景 李阳
装帧设计：熊晓莹 宋索迪
设计制作：宋微微

出版发行：五洲传播出版社
地　　址：北京市海淀区北小马厂6号华天大厦
邮　　编：100038
网　　址：www.cicc.org.cn
电　　话：010－58891281
印　　刷：恒美印务（广州）有限公司
开　　本：100×185mm　1/32
印　　张：4.875
版　　次：2009年1月第1版 2009年1月第1次印刷
06800（平）

Foreword

All journeys have secret destinations of which the traveler is unaware.

Martin Buber, German philosopher

It may seem odd to begin a guide on the right purchase of different types of embroidery with a quote about traveling, but traveling is an indispensable part of the Western experience of China. For thousands of years, the West's knowledge of China has not been a story told by Chinese people themselves, but were experiences narrated by the visiting travelers.

As a result, the Western imagination of the Middle Kingdom has often taken on a fascinating, and at times, fantastical edge. The tendency to misinform, exaggerate, or simply make things up was exacerbated by the vast distance that was covered en route to access this distant and exotic land. This Oriental awe was also magnified by the mysterious valuables that made its way through different cultures, religions, and kingdoms, in places as far as Western Europe, before reaching their final destinations.

China, 中国 "Zhong guo" means "middle kingdom". It gives the outsider some idea as to where the Chinese had traditionally placed themselves on the map. Furthermore, the incredibly rich indigenous culture is replete with practices and beliefs. These were not known by the outside world for thousands of years. This isolationism continues. Perhaps, it was not until the recent years that there has been any real effort by the Chinese to communicate with the outside world.

Since time immemorial, silk has been a jealously guarded secret in China, and remained a highly prized tradable good, as far as Europe in the west.

Perhaps it is the intransigence of the Chinese that makes the Middle Kingdom so magnetically attractive to the Western imagination. It is a possible hangover from the wonderful, mysterious treasures that used to travel thousands of miles along the Silk Road. Perhaps it is because of the fact the country has long been difficult to access for the outsiders. Perhaps today it is a combination of these aspects, along with an admiration for the country's fast economic development

Modern China looks like it is adopting Western ways. From Western technology and medicine, to KFC, Adidas, and basketball, China seems to be a country moving away from its historical and cultural legacy at a breakneck speed. However, deep within, the cultural gap between the East and the West remains vast.

Even in interpersonal communications, cultural mannerisms present a number of barriers to effective communication, not to mention the disparity of language. Although we now have the ability to fly to China from anywhere in the world within a few hours, developing a mutual understanding of the inherent differences, still has a long way to go.

Furthermore, it could be argued that China is not moving away from its historical legacy due to its present, swift economic transformation, but is journeying back toward it. Throughout history, the Middle Kingdom has been one of the world's most powerful economic and cultural middle points, even if in Western history books express awe over its distance and inaccessibility. With an economy that has grown at 10 percent for 30 years, a netizen population that has already overtaken the United States in terms of numbers, well over half a billion mobile phones, and an inexhaustible supply of cheap labor; the Chinese economic juggernaut is going to roll on for quite some time to come.

My own journey to China began, without me being quite aware of it, about 10 years ago when I began a degree in Asian Studies. I had yet not decided what I wanted to do in life. After battling through to graduation, I was still none the wiser! Through a combination of luck and fate I found myself teaching English in Taiwan. After a short time in Taiwan, I realized that my future did not lie in teaching, but I was still at a loss as to where exactly it should be. I had already begun studying Chinese at this stage, and after a year and a half in the classroom, something snapped inside me and I decided to dedicate myself to the full-time study of the language.

Your journey to China may consist of a two-week trip through the great cultural and economic centers of the country. You may be a long-term China resident with no plans to head to your country of origin, any time soon. Or it may so be that the journey you are undertaking in China now has a secret destination chartered for you that you are unaware of at present.

Since we began this introduction with the thought of a European philosopher, it seems only fitting to conclude it with a quote of Chinese wisdom. A quote that works on a metaphysical and practical level, and is as applicable to traveling and pondering upon the deeper meaning of life as it is to, well, appreciating the world of Chinese embroidery.

A good traveler has no fixed plans, and is not intent on arriving.

Lao Zi, Taoist sage.

Rhys Wesley

Contents

How to Select series is jointly published by Marshall Cavendish and China Intercontinental Press in 2008. The advices given in the series are Independent. No advertising arrangement has been involved. No payment has been accepted by the publishers for listing or introducing any business. The authors of the series have not accepted any discount or payment in exchange for any positive coverage either. The authors and publishers have taken all reasonable care in preparing the series, we disclaim all liability arising from using the series.

《如何选购》系列由五洲传播出版社和名创出版集团于2008年合作出版，书中的有关建议是独立的，没有涉及任何广告安排。出版社未向书中介绍或者列名的任何商家索取报酬。本系列的作者也未曾因对商家进行正面报道而接受商家的折扣优惠或酬谢。在本系列图书出版准备过程中，作者和出版社均已尽最大努力做到客观、中立，我们对使用本系列图书出现的问题概不予负责。

Why Embroidery?

Welcome to the world of embroidery: A glance inside an embroidery store.
(Photographed in White Peacock Art World).

Is this your first visit to China? Maybe you have been living here for many years. Whether you are a long-term resident or a flying visitor, everyone who visits China looks, at some stage, for a piece of treasure that captures the essence of this ancient culture.

I'm not talking about a typical piece of electronics. If you are looking for something enduring, practical, relatively affordable, and unique to China, then I suggest embroidery.

Legends and Truth

When I first arrived in China, 3 years ago, I was mesmerised by the stunning embroidery products on display in the market at Wangfujing, Beijing. What particularly caught my eye on that first day were the extraordinarily life-like tigers lounging indolently on the wall hangings. Delving further into the back corners of small stores I was amazed at the variety of embroidered goods that could be found. Fancying myself as a bit of a China buff, I became determined to find out more. The question uppermost on my mind was how and where did this fantastic art form originate?

The first thing you will learn about China is that everything is several thousand years old. Embroidery is no exception. And like all ancient things, there are many legends about its origin. The following is my favorite.

In ancient times, the people in humid, tropical southern China experienced one water-borne disaster after another. Typhoons, floods, storms, and tempests unleashed their fury and wreaked terrible vengeance upon the land. The people experienced untold suffering. In despair, they turned to the dragon god — master of the sea and the water, for protection. To display their devotion, they tattooed their bodies with fantastic images of dragons. Sounds painful, doesn't it? I'd probably stick with the storms and tempests!

◆ *Lion: King of the beasts! (Provided by Goulswon)*

Concerned for his people's welfare, or perhaps unable to endure the pain himself of having thousands of needles stuck into his body, a tribal chieftain named Zhong Yong organized a meeting to discuss possible alternatives to tattooing. Wise and venerable scholars, priests, and shamans gathered to chew the fat. Zhong Yong's granddaughter was also sitting in the room, eavesdropping on their conversation as she sewed. She was so fascinated by the conversation that she lost focus on her sewing. The needle slipped and punctured her skin. Blood dripped onto the cloth. Gasping with pain, Zhong Yong's granddaughter stared intently at the blood as it spread over her sewing. Slowly an idea began to unfold in her mind. For seven days and seven nights she labored intensively. When she was ready, she presented her creation to her grandfather. The chief was amazed. His granddaughter had tattooed the sacred dragon image directly onto his clothes!

On an auspicious day, the chief convened a tribal meeting and proudly displayed his beautiful new outfit. "From this day forward," he proclaimed to the tribe, "we will no longer tattoo our bodies." Inwardly he may have breathed a sigh of relief!

As for his granddaughter, she is remembered to this day. A style of needlework, Nü Hong (女红), was named after her.

The legend lives: Nü Hong-style embroidered dress.

Is it just me, or does inventing tattooing before embroidery sound a trifle sadistic to you too?

However romantic the legend of Zhong Yong and his astute granddaughter may be, I cannot claim it to be 100 percent accurate. I will give a more prosaic explanation with a little more "objectivity" and with some "historical facts." Of course, any introduction to Chinese art of embroidery cannot be separated from silk. Silk, famed as one of China's

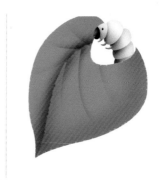

Stunning silk: Silkworms began to be bred more than 4,000 years ago.

most enduring gifts to the world, is thought to have first been cultivated somewhere between 5000 and 3000 B.C., making it older than your grandma! Although experts are still unsure of the exact time period in which embroidery emerged, a cloth embroidered with dragons, phoenixes, and tigers was unearthed in a tomb from the period of the Warring States (475 B.C.–221 B.C.).

(One thing you will learn about China is that everything happened at least 2,000 years ago!)

Silk is so light and so strong it was actually used by Mongols as a kind of armor. The strength of the fibres meant that it would reduce the chance of arrows puncturing the skin, thus reducing the possibility of infection. However, chances are, if you got hit by an arrow wearing your silk top at the Forbidden City, praising its protective qualities is probably going to be the last thing on your mind!

The Art of the Needle

Long after Nü Hong, during the period of the Three Kingdoms (A.D.220 – A.D.280), a woman once again provided an artistic

---

Multitalented: A top-notch embroiderer usually is a painter too.

and practical leap in the development of embroidery. However, this legend also involves a powerful man.

The King of Wu, Sun Quan, was a man known for his efficiency.

At the time of his reign, China was wrecked by civil unrest. As a preparation for war, Sun Quan wanted to find a painter with great skill and keen observation of detail to represent every available mountain, river, road, forest, and village in a single illustration. (He was a man of unreasonable demands!) The prime minister, in a true spirit of nepotism, recommended his young daughter for the job. The girl made a detailed sketch for the king, but as she was working, she paused and reflected on the disadvantages of using paper for such a valuable document. Paper could easily be destroyed by hand and ruined by water. In a flash of inspiration, she decided to embroider the entire map. So impressed was the king that he called her a "goddess of the needle." Incidentally, she is also recorded as the first female painter in Chinese history, thus demonstrating once again the

A Song Dynasty scroll: Truly the work of a needle goddess. (Provided by Goulswon).

age-old link between the arts of painting and embroidery in this country.

Personally, the rapturous colors and amazing animals on display in an average work of Chinese embroidery leave Western embroidery for dead. But in the interests of objectivity, I think it's a good idea to take a look at some of the things that make the two styles different.

Chinese embroidery is known as "free embroidery." It is a form of "surface" embroidery, which is where the patterns and stitches are laid on top of the canvas, rather than stitched through it. That is to say, it is the opposite of counted-thread embroidery. European styles of embroidery include both counted-thread (such as cross stitch, needlepoint) and free styles (such as crewel, as used in the Bayeux Tapestry, which narrates the tale of the Norman invasion of England).

Besides technique, materials used are, of course, the major difference between Chinese and Western embroidery. Since Europeans did not develop a tradition of breeding silkworms, they never developed the knowledge of how to use silk thread and cloth for the purposes of embroidery.

A Valuable Investment

Have you spent a fortune on buying clothes, electronics, and DVDs? The average visitor shopping in China today is like a kid in a candy store, with endless treats and eager sales people everywhere! It's easy to spot a Westerner with limited time in this country. Their arms are full of bags, eyes crazed with consumer lust, and fingers are perpetually hovering at their

Musical Fairy: This is an image from the Buddhist Mogao Grotto. (Provided by Goulswon).

coming to a slow but inevitable end. New opportunities help the Chinese people add value to their education and find professional jobs. The young generation keen on fast growth are leaving labor-intensive ones. Inevitably, the price of unique products, such as embroidery, will increase as less people will be willing to spend time and labor on this. Again the slow but sure appreciation of the Chinese yuan against the U.S. dollar will add to the increase.

hip pocket! With the opening up of the country in the late 1970s, China has played host to an ever-increasing number of tourists and outside influences. But this is not necessarily going to last forever, especially for unique Chinese goods such as embroidery.

With more and more techniques for mass production being developed all the time, coupled with China's breakneck economic growth, the days of cheap, handmade traditional Chinese embroidery purchased straight from the source are

A Cultural Gift to the World

Right now shopping in China is a party for visitors, and it's tempting to grab as much on offer as possible. Clothes, DVDs, and electronics are just some of the goods that can be found cheaper in China than many other countries. And hey, why not enjoy these kinds of things?

But buying Chinese embroidery has more to it than just the economic concerns. Embroidery is used in innumerable ways. If you will allow me a pause to take a breath, I will unleash upon you just some of the wide-ranging practical and decorative goods that enterprising and astute Chinese artists have made. Take a deep breath...

Wallets, shoes, silk greeting cards, handkerchiefs, handbags, lingerie, cup mats, chair covers, sofa covers, cushion covers, curtains, fans, scarves, backs for mirrors, pillow covers, parachutes (yes, parachutes!), bathrobes, and those beautiful, traditional female dresses, the qi pao, shirts, trousers...

Apart from this, embroidery can of course be appreciated as a piece of artwork in its own right, as wall hangings, etc.

When you buy a handcrafted piece of Chinese embroidery, you are buying a piece that is one of China's greatest cultural gifts to the world. As the character for embroidery suggests, the ancient Chinese themselves thought extremely highly of its intrinsic beauty. So highly, in fact, that originally it was considered too extraordinary to play a part in the lives of ordinary people. Only the emperor and his immediate family were permitted to wear it.

And as Buddhism flourished in China during the Wei, Jin, Sui, and Tang dynasties, Buddhist sutras images of Buddhist statues were embroidered onto silk to help offer spiritual guidance to the soul.

Chinese silk embroidery has been a medium to express religious piety and capitalist greed. It has

Practical delights: A snapshot of a store for everyday-use embroidered work. (Photographed in the Gongmei Building at Wangfujing).

Enter the dragon: A luxurious, embroidered robe.

traveled through deserts on the backs of camels and in first-class airplane cabins. Although it is a Chinese invention, as recognized universally, it is appreciated all around the globe. It is at once tough, durable, pleasing to the eye, and soft to the touch. Despite its historic value, this visually ecstatic representation of one of the world's most rich and enduring cultures is easily affordable to overseas visitors.

Is there any other art form with such an incredible pedigree?

My advice to you folks, is to ride the silk embroidery bandwagon while you have this chance.

The Silk Road Continues...

For centuries, the aristocrats of Europe spent huge sums of money on this mysterious fabric that came from a distant land far to the east. In fact, it was so highly prized that the overland trading routes between China and Europe became known (in both China and Europe) as the Silk Road (丝绸之路).

So long: No more desert treks on camels.

The Silk Road was a testament to the allure this wonderful art form held for Westerners. And it is worth noting that although silk traveled out of China, European embroidery did not travel "in." It would be interesting to know what an ancient Chinese master of embroidery would have made of Western embroidery materials and techniques.

unlike flares, demand for silk remained strong, and trade continued.

In this way, people today are very lucky, because it only takes hours to come to China and have access to these beautiful works of art. Farewell, long journeys on leaky, wooden boats!

This is quite ironic, considering it was (a) not a road as such, and (b) carried numerous goods besides silk. Following Vasco da Gama's voyage to India around Africa, the Silk Road, like flares, went out of fashion. However

Farewell, dusty journeys on camels! However, some things have not changed. Like the ancient traders on the long Silk Road, buying embroidery in China is an occasion for intense, but exciting, haggling.

A Fabulous Show

Xiù (绣) is the Chinese character for embroidery. This character is made up of two parts, known as "radicals." This character contains in it a clue to how important silk is with regards to embroidery in the minds of Chinese. The left hand radical comes from the character for silk, 丝 (pronounced sī). The right hand radical, 秀 (pronounced xiù), means "elegant," or "beautiful." So written Chinese contains in it something of the esteem in which this art form is held.

Pretty nifty, eh? If you want to impress a vendor that you have some understanding of the culture and history associated with different styles of Chinese embroidery, it never hurts to use these terms. However, be sure you are familiar with how to read pinyin (the phonetic transliteration of Chinese). Finally, yet importantly, pay attention to the tones!

Chinese calligraphy: The character '绣' (embroidery).

Four Beauties of the Embroidery Family

From four different areas of China four distinct styles of silk embroidery have developed. These "Big Four" main styles are known as Sū Xiù(苏绣), Xiāng Xiù (湘绣), Yuè Xiù (粤绣), and Shǔ Xiù(蜀绣). The following is a brief guide to these four major schools of embroidery:

Su Xiu (苏绣)

Feeling cultural? Su Xiu is also known as Sūzhōu embroidery, amazingly also the city from which it hails. Sūzhōu is an eastern city filled with rippling water and lustrous silk, which is reflected in the multiple folds in their rivers and silk works. Sūzhōu won the title of "City of Embroidery" in the Qing dynasty (A.D.1616–1911), making it the toughest and meanest embroidery in the world at the time. However it was in the Song Dynasty (A.D.960–1279) that Su Xiu became popular, along with the use of the first government-issued banknotes in world history. (They must have got tired of carrying all their gold around!)

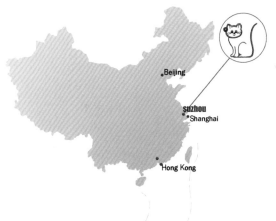

Silky streets: Suzhou.

At some distant point of antiquity, it was recorded that the embroidery street in Sūzhōu was known as "Silk Thread Lane." According to ancient records, "Every household is engaged in embroidering, and every family has embroidery girls." The records claimed the artists of the time to be so skilled that they were able to create up to 700 shades of color, which must have made Sūzhōu look the equal of a Mardi Gras celebration!

During the period of the Republic of China (1912–1949) Su Xiu embroidery

went into decline as a result of the civil wars that rocked the country, although it has since regained some popularity.

Su Xiu embroidery is acclaimed for its detailed and intricate representations of natural scenery and human figures.

Embroidered painting: Vincent Van Gogh's Green Wheat Field with Cypress. (Provided by Guanzhe)

A distinctive feature is that it is sometimes double sided, with the same picture being represented on both sides, with some variation. When I first saw a double-side embroidered cat in a shop in Wángfǔjǐng, I was very surprised. On one side there was a black and white cat, but on the other it was yellow and white. That's right! I've never seen a yellow and white cat either. Someone told me that on a single piece of silk Suzhou artists can embroider pictures of the Five Sacred Mountains, rivers and seas, cities, and furious battles. This may or may not be an exaggeration, but

Still life: A great home decoration.
(Provided by Goulswon)

there is a Chinese saying: "All the countries in the world could be embroidered on one piece of Suzhou brocade."

Su Xiu embroidery's complexity and the fact that it uses silk thread on silk backing make it the fine wine of Chinese embroidery. And like fine wine, it just keeps getting better with age. Many of the best pieces still in existence are hundreds of years old, including clothing, wall hangings, and even intricate book covers! As such, a well-made piece of Su embroidery is a good, future investment as well as a decorative or practical purchase for now. Bottoms up!

Traditional human figure embroidery: A girl playing with a parrot. (Photographed in White Peacock Art World)

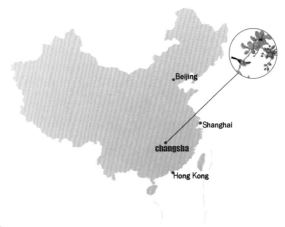

The journey continues: Changsha.

Xiang Xiu（湘绣）

Feeling rebellious? Due to the lack of precision with regards to the needlework, do as you please creations of the artists, and impressive longevity, Xiang Xiu embroidery is the Rolling Stones of the Chinese embroidery world. It comes from the central southern province of Húnán, and especially from the city of Chángshā. Possible the most ancient of the four main styles, the earliest example of Xiang Xiu was found in a Han dynasty (206 B.C.–

A.D. 220) tomb. Incredibly, the techniques used in Xiang Xiu are very similar to those used today. This consistency is yet another reason to invite comparisons with the ancient rockers.

Through the Qing dynasty, Xiang Xiu enjoyed something

Guardian of the house: A roaring lion. (Provided by Zaihong)

of a renaissance. Over time, it also borrowed many stylistic elements from Su Xiu and Yue Xiu embroidery methods, which has led some scholars to identify this period as the true birth of Xiang Xiu. However, there is no doubt that it possesses many unique characteristics. By the end of the Qing dynasty, as well as in the early period of the Republic of China, it was the most popular style of Chinese embroidery around. This proves that if you keep getting gigs it is only a matter of time before you are fashionable with the young set again.

Many designs are copied from paintings; however, they have also been borrowed from engraving and calligraphy. Common themes are landscapes, people, flowers, birds, and other animals especially the ferocious tigers, you may see strolling with quiet menace around the shop floor.

Xiang Xiu embroidery is often done on both sides of transparent chiffon silk. It uses pure silk, hard satin, soft satin, and nylon as materials. Both practical and aesthetic items are made in this style. The most beautiful are valuable works of art and, like reunion tour concert tickets, are ideal as expensive gifts, but better for personal use. Xiang Xiu embroidery is especially popular in the west.

Impressed observers have noticed that sometimes the animals and people depicted in Xiang Xiu embroidery seem almost to be breathing. Don't worry! This is not due to anything you might have ingested before the show. The bright colors and thick stitching sometimes manage to create this impression.

Natural themes: Two birds on a Yulan flower.
(Provided by Zaihong)

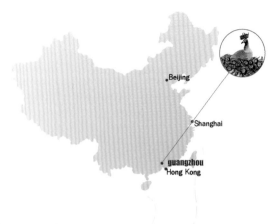

The summery south: Guangdong.

Yue Xiu（粤绣）

See yourself as a free spirit? Yue embroidery is for you. More eclectic and offbeat than its cousins, Yue Xiu embroidery is the hippy love child of the Chinese embroidery world. It comes from Guǎngdōng in the far south of China, around what is today Hong Kong. Not coincidentally, Yue Xiu embroidery rose to prominence in the Tang dynasty (A.D.618–907), which was to Imperial China what the '60s were to 20th century America.

The bright colors and variety of different threads ensured that the Yue Xiu summer of embroidered love lasted for several hundred years. (Imagine that!) Early practitioners used exotic materials such as peacock feathers to make a colorful thread. This can still be found today. Perhaps less attractively, hair from horsetails is also used.

Yue Xiu embroidery was further refined during the Ming dynasty,

The delight of flight: A butterfly falls in love with a tulip. (Provided by Chen Shaofang)

in which it developed into an important folk handicraft industry. In 1514, an enterprising Portuguese merchant bought an embroidered dragon robe in Guǎngzhōu and took it back as a gift to his king. This started a European craze for Yue Xiu embroidery, with large amounts of it bought by Western traders every year. Such was its popularity that Western monarchs and even depictions of Jesus were embroidered in the Yue Xiu style.

True to its hippy spirit, favorite designs are based around worship of the sun, birds, dragons, and phoenixes. Its stitching style has been called "complicated and crowded in patterns, brilliant in colors, simple in stitch, rough and loose in embroidery threads with irregularly long and short stitches and overlapped patterns." Perhaps being carried away with their own spirit of carefree abandon, practitioners sometimes use gold and silver thread in their works to create a three-dimensional impression. Small circles are stitched in straight lines, with knots periodically tied for a more dramatic effect. Because of this it has also been called Golden Circle embroidery. Due to the geographical position of where it originated on the south coast, maritime scenes are also used.

In the typically grandiose style of Chinese prose, a common theme of Yue Xiu embroidery is "A Hundred Birds Paying Homage to the Phoenix." Oh the things I'd do for such adulation...!

Yue Xiu embroidery can be subcategorized into "Guang" and "Chao" styles, both of which have their own stitching techniques. It is especially popular in Hong Kong and Macau, but also much loved by Ming and Qing dynasty emperors in Beijing. If you visit the Forbidden City today, you will get the chance to see a

Themes of auspiciousness: Golden dragon and silver phoenix. (Photographed in White Peacock Art World)

large collection of outstanding Yue Xiu embroidery and engage in a little embroidered love.

Shu Xiu （蜀绣）

Feeling a little more elegant? Think that Yue Xiu embroidery sounds too carefree? Shu Xiu embroidery is its cultivated cousin.

Shu Xiu is also known as Chuan embroidery, by virtue of the fact it comes from the western part of Sìchuān province. (In Chinese Si 四 and Chuan 川 are two different characters.) In fact, Shu is itself an ancient name for Sichuan Province. It too, has an ancient history and along with

paper, steel, and the dawn of the Silk Road come to us courtesy those eager beavers from the Han Dynasty. They also invented something called the armillary sphere, which means they were smart. So important was Shu Xiu embroidery to contemporaries in the Han dynasty era that in true bureaucratic style the government set up an office to deal with its administration. Need there be any more evidence of how seriously the Chinese take this art form?

However it was not until the Song dynasty (A.D.960–1279) that Shu Xiu embroidery really took off, once again proving that if you hang around long enough the law of averages means that you have to be considered cool by someone. At this point

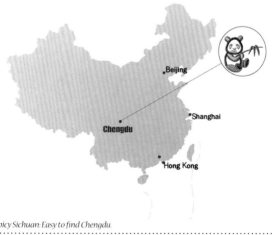

Spicy Sichuan: Easy to find Chengdu.

in time Shu Xiu surpassed all others as the preeminent form of embroidery in China.

Shu embroidery incorporates flowers, leaves, animals, human portraits, and, coming from the stunning high-altitude province of Sìchuān, rivers and mountains as its themes. Also due to the fact it hails from Sìchuān, pandas are one of the animals often found in this kind of embroidery. An ancient text, "The History

Shu Xiu: The cultured cousin in the embroidery family.

of Dongyang Kingdom" called Shu Xiu embroidery one of the two treasures of Middle Sìchuān. Unlike the rebellious spirit of rock evident in Xiang Xiu embroidery, Shu Xiu stitches are neat and even. Colors are elegantly arranged.

After the founding of the People's Republic of China, Shu Xiu embroidery once again enjoyed resurgence as modern techniques were used and new factories were set up. There are at least 100 stitching techniques in this wonderfully complex form of embroidery.

If you are looking for themes of auspicious happiness, then Shu Xiu embroidery may be the style for you. Probably the most famous example of Shu Xiu embroidery is the massive "Lotus and Carp" hanging in the Sichuan Hall, Great Hall of the People.

Unfortunately, there are not many ancient examples of Shu Xiu embroidery left, although pieces of work from Jin dynasty (A.D.1115–1234) do survive at Southwest Normal University. This piece was embroidered on a piece of damask silk and features a rooster standing on an island. It is raising its head and extending its wings in the direction of the rising sun. This piece carries the royal seal of Emperor Zhangzong. And if that's not cultured enough, then you're too hard to please!

Jing Xiu （京绣）

Note to all the bored husbands and boyfriends out there: if the femininity of embroidery is getting too much for you, look no further than Jing Xiu, the most masculine of all embroidery forms. Not only is it the only form practiced by men, Jing Xiu was the style worn by the emperor. Thus Jing Xiu embroidery includes many testosterone-laden symbols such as dragons and phoenixes. Although it was first developed in the Tang Dynasty, along with Yue embroidery, Jing Xiu is far more dignified than its hippy cousin.

Due to the fact it was made for nobility, Jing Xiu was often made more for decorative and ceremonial purposes rather than practical ones.

Miao Xiu （苗绣）

Did you know that China is home to 56 ethnic groups? Han Chinese consist of 94 percent of the population and are by

Themes of love: A Jing Xiu handbag. (Photographed in Jingxiu Shop)

far the largest. Some of the smaller ethnic groups are well-known by Westerners, for example Tibetans, but many are in the spotlight far less. Because of this the average visitor to China may even forget they exist. It is a shame considering the wonderful art they have to offer.

More Miao magic: This can be used as a decorative wall hanging. (Photographed in Pan Yuzhen's home)

One such group is the Miao, from the southwest provinces of China.

This Miao woman, Pan Yuzhen, was born in Guizhou province. She sells ancient Miao pieces and ornaments from other ethnic groups, and has participated in exhibitions in Hong Kong, Singapore, and United States. (Photo provided by Pan Yuzhen)

These people have their own rich language, culture and stories, which has in turn inspired their own practices of embroidery. This is one of their stories.

Long before man existed, a butterfly flew out of the trunk of a maple tree. She fell in love with a drop of water in a field, and they gave birth to 12 eggs, out of which millions of things were born, including man. So according to Miao cultural beliefs, this special butterfly is the creator of all things, and they call her "Mother Butterfly." Because of this, butterflies are a common theme of

An embroidered environment: An embroiderer in an embroidered dress doing embroidery.

Traditionally, all women were accomplished embroidery practitioners.

Although they have not reached the international recognition of the "Big Four" styles of embroidery, examples can nonetheless be found in museums and collections around the world. Because in recent years the amount of skilled artists practicing Miao embroidery has been steadily diminishing, an organization known as "Weng Liu Miao Camp" has been collecting art works for some years, some dating back to the Ming Dynasty.

their embroidery work. It's a nice story, isn't it?

The Miao people often embroidered historical scenes, mythological beliefs, and images from even their surrounding environment onto their clothing and art. It has even been said that Miao embroidery is like a historical text without the written word. However, it has appeared in written Chinese texts since the Tang Dynasty.

As for what it looks like, in Miao embroidery the main colors used are red and green, which are supplemented by other colors.

One of the most commonly used techniques in Miao embroidery is called "Flat Embroidery." Shapes and lines are often exaggerated according to the spontaneous wishes of the creator. However, symmetry is quite an important aspect.

On horseback: Traditionally, one of the functions of horsetail embroidery was to make a carrier to hold babies on one's back. (Photographed in Pan Yuzhen's home)

Horsepower: Horsetail embroidery is surprisingly attractive and strong.

Horsetail Embroidery

Bored of the same old embroidery routine? Check this out. Guìzhōu province's Shui ethnic group makes embroidery out of horsetails, after they eat the horse (just joking!). Horse tail embroidery can be found on clothes, shoes, wallets, and bags. However this skill is fast being lost as young women are moving to the cities to enhance their professional and education opportunities.

This kind of embroidery is labor-intensive — a dress may take more than a month to complete. This is due to the process of embroidery. To make this kind of pattern, three thin threads are entwined into three or four strands of horse tail. After that cross-stitches is used to embroider a piece. This increases the price. A good quality, hand-embroidered dress may cost up to 10,000 yuan. However, because it's a skill that may disappear, now is a great time to buy!

Embroidery Process

Are you the type of person who enjoys embroidery itself, or are you the type who enjoys buying the finished product without the effort? If you would identify yourself with the second group, then you are with me. And if you are in the first group, I have nothing but respect for you. Having tried (with modest success) at this art form myself, I can still give you some helpful, handy hints on how to handpick material. Also, if you don't want to try embroidering yourself, having an understanding of the materials and techniques involved may help you come to a decision as to what you like in embroidered art. Like the preparation of fine food, the ingredients of embroidered art are critical.

Ingredients for an Embroidery Recipe

Fabrics

The first stop is fabrics. Let's take a gander.

Although historically speaking silk has been considered the most sought after material both in and outside China, do not be fooled that it is the only one available. Far from it. Today you can easily find embroidered burlap, velvet, damask, organdy, wool, gingham, ticking, batiste, denim, and twill.

Complex work: An embroidery art piece with tens of thousands stitches.

Obviously, this is a lot of materials to choose from, but the type you want will depend on what kind of embroidery you are doing. These are some points to consider:

Some examples of tightly woven fabrics are cotton, aida, wool, and linen.

Some of the most commonly used fabrics for embroidery are linen, calico, cotton velvet, satin, and our old friend, silk.

Think about the type of finish you want. A matt finish is duller and unreflective, but better for complicated scenes. Shiny finishes are better for foreground and background contrast.

Funky fabrics: From the drawing board to the finished product.

How heavy will your finished piece be? It is important that the material can support the weight of the embroidered product. This will depend on what you are embroidering. Something complex is likely to be heavier. Also, items like bows and ribbons will add to the overall weight.

What kind of stitch will you use? Again, the type of stitch you want to use will affect your choice of fabric. Complex stitching such as elaborate flora and fauna will make your finished product heavier. You will therefore need a heavier backing material to support its weight.

Threads

What kind of thread will you use? Thread will also make a difference to how heavy your finished product will be. Furthermore, the thread should not permit the fabric to be visible from the front of your embroidered piece. The weave of the fabric should be such that the thread can pass through it easily.

Assess the strength of the weave before you make a purchase.

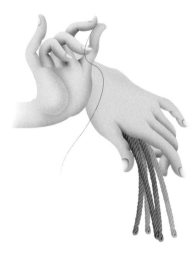

Top threads: The selection process is crucial.

It must be strong enough to ensure the threads are held in place. Thicker threads demand a looser weave.

Make sure threads used contrast well with the fabric and are prominent on it.

Needles

Painters use different paint-brushes for different purposes, and so do embroiderers. The type of thread, fabric, and embroidery technique will affect what kind of needle is most suited to your project.

The most commonly available needles are crewel, chenille, and tapestry. Crewel needles are short with a long, slim eye, and sharp point. Chenille needles are similar but larger. Tapestry needles have a blunt tip.

Remember that sharp crewel and chenille needles are more suitable for projects requiring you to stitch through the material. Blunt-tipped tapestry needles are better for working in the top threads of fabric, such as in huck embroidery.

Check out the size of the needle. All three types come in various numbered sizes, but the higher the number, the finer the needle.

The next step is to match the needle to your thread size. To ensure maximum efficiency, the most suitable size of needle is one that is only slightly thicker at the eye than the needle of your thread. This will mean that the needle will make a hole for the thread only slightly thicker than the thread itself, enabling it to pass through easily.

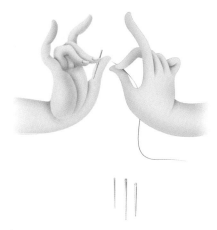

you can work, however standard lap hoops, which range in diameter from 4–12 inches are relatively easy to move. They are also cheaper. In China, many craftsmen have traditionally used one made of wood, which they stand on the ground. Although it looks like a machine used for torture, it is a very effective tool, albeit pretty big to pack in suitcases.

A pointed selection: Make sure you choose carefully.

And remember: a shorter needle is usually easier to work with, however using too small a needle may cause your thread to break. Conversely, if you use too large a needle, it may be difficult to keep your stitches even.

Extra accessories: Small embroidery hoops and a big wooden one.

Hoops

Hoop, hoop a loop, hoop a loop! This is as important to embroidery as your keys are to your car. Well, maybe not, actually. That would be the needle. But anyway, your hoop (plastic or metal) holds the fabric taut during the embroidery process. The bigger the hoop, the bigger the area over which

Scissors

As embroidery deals with small details, precision is a must. When shopping for scissors, think small and sharp. Real sharp! Stainless steel is the best.

Preparation for the embroidery cook-up

Ok, we have finished shopping for our big embroidery cook-up and are now ready for the preparation itself. Actually, the shopping is pretty straightforward. It's the embroidery itself that gets tricky.

The embroidery techniques used today come to us courtesy of countless generations of Chinese women engaging in this craft over thousands of years. Due to the patriarchal conventions of traditional Chinese society, embroidery was one of the few ways women could gain status and recognition.

The efforts of these women as a sum total are quite mind-boggling. Over the centuries an almost superhuman level of patience has been required by an extraordinarily large number of embroiderers. Even today, a small, high-quality piece of embroidered art can take several months to complete. A large work of similar quality may take up to several years, and involve many embroiderers. Do you think you would have the patience to sit in a room for the best part of your life making tiny stitch after tiny stitch?

Furthermore, because many embroidered products are based on paintings, a skilled embroiderer must have some knowledge of painting patterns. It has been argued with considerable persuasiveness that embroidery is more difficult than painting, because every brush stroke may take thousands of stitches.

Ok now, eager embroidery chefs! Onto the preparation!

Feminine mystique: Through Chinese history, embroidery has been a woman's job.

Understanding the Process

◆ *Place the fabric on the frame.*

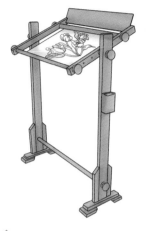

◆ *Draw the pattern onto the fabric.*

◆ *Select needles, threads.*

◆ *The process itself.*

Embroidery is challenging but very rewarding to do. After taking a look at the whole process, we should also learn a few stitches to appreciate the complexity of the work and the time that goes into it. It is with the individual stitches that

◆ *The fantastic finished product.*

these complicated mythological tales have been expressed by countless embroidery masters. You can practice on heavy, dark material such as linen. Use light colored thread for the best effect. In the meantime, allow the chef, (moi) to introduce you to stitching lingo 101. Bear in mind that although many of these stitches are simple to execute by themselves, when they are combined with each other the results can be very complex. Ready, steady, stitch!

Straight stitch （直针）

The "straight" stitch is the basic unit of sewing and embroidery. All other stitches are derived from it. It is the simple method that you probably learnt in primary school of pulling the needle in and out along a line in the fabric. Although simple, it's an important part of many traditional embroidery techniques.

Nail stitch （钉针）

This stitch is extremely simple to work. (Good news, right?) First a heavy thread is brought up behind the fabric with a large eye needle. The surface thread is laid on the fabric, and then anchored by a second finer thread. Small, straight stitches are taken over the thick thread and back through the fabric. Work along the thick thread until the line is completed. Take the heavy thread to the back of the fabric with a large needle and secure both ends of the heavy thread by using a few small stitches. The second thread can be arranged in patterns, as inlaid work.

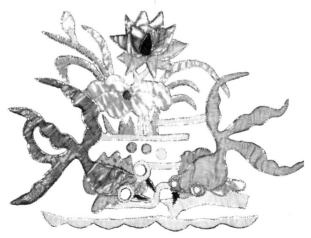

Straight stitch.

Roll stitch （挽针）

The roll stitch is beautiful, decorative and tricky! It is accomplished by performing lots and lots of yarn overs before drawing through the yarn to complete the stitch. The tricky part is getting your hook to glide smoothly through all of those yarn overs.

🔹 *Roll stitch.*

Chain stitch （锁针）

Ok, now you're getting clever. To execute a chain stitch, you pull the thread up from behind the fabric, and then push the needle back down exactly the same hole. A certain distance from the stitch, and before the loop completely disappears, the needle comes back up and through the loop. This prevents it from being pulled completely out. The needle is then passed through to the back of the fabric again before the whole process is repeated. A Lazy-daisy stitch is an example of a chain stitch, however, in this the loop stitch is held by a tiny tacking stitch at the tip. A Spanish Chain or Zig-Zag Chain is also an example.

Seed stitch （打籽针）

Although I like it, the seed stitch is one that some people love and some people tend to hate. Those who don't like it usually complain about all the switching between knits and purls, but that is what gives this pattern its texture. Works on multiples of two stitches — row one: knit one, purl one across; row two: purl one, knit one across. Repeat these two rows for pattern. This stitch is called as "dǎzi" stitch in pinyin, which often used images depicting the wish for sons, such as a child emerging from a pomegranate. A dazi is a pun on sons and hence the double meaning being...

Although a vast amount of knowledge has been passed down through time, much of what we know today about traditional Chinese embroidery is due to the efforts of two people early in the 20th century. At the time China was already undergoing quite cataclysmic change, but not to the extent that it was to during the violent eruptions of civil war and Japanese invasion in later decades. Before this happened, in 1918,

Seed stitch.

the first modern treatise on embroidery was published. The invaluable cultural and historical information contained within it was the result of collaboration between Shen Shou, a famous female embroidery master, and Zhang Jian, a wealthy industrialist. Shen Shou rose to prominence when she presented the Empress Dowager Ci Xi with an embroidered tapestry representing "Eight Immortals Celebrating Birthday." In 1915 she entered an award-winning work depicting Jesus at the World Expo.

However, despite her vast talents and knowledge, Shen Shou was plagued by poor health. It took the dedicated assistance of the wealthy, embroidery and art-loving Zhang Jian to get the book written. At the time of writing, Zhang Jian was a successful entrepreneur in his 60s and Shen Shou a bedridden woman in her 40s. So passionate was Zhang about preserving the knowledge of this master of the art of embroidery that he volunteered to sit beside her bed and listen to her dictate the content of the book. What makes this story all the more remarkable is that a man as powerful and successful as Zhang Jian listened to a humble woman. This goes totally against the patriarchal slant of traditional Chinese society. Like the ancient legend of Nü Hong, and the only slightly less distant figure of the daughter of the prime minister of the Wu Kingdom thousands of years before, it was a woman who held the ancient knowledge of embroidery and transmitted it to the modern era.

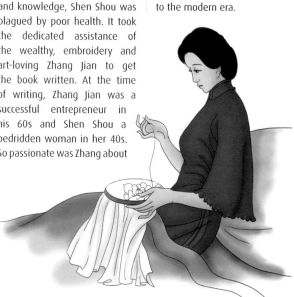

Dedicated artist: Shen Shou worked on her bed even when in ill health.

Add Auspicious Elements

Chinese is a wonderfully subtle language! Did you know that there are approximately 400 different sounding syllables in Chinese (1600 if you include tones), compared to over 10,000 in English? This has given rise to a rich culture of puns based on homophones. So rich, in fact, that it has even penetrated Chinese art.

Some amazing examples homophone-based puns can be found in classical embroidery. Consider these examples:

If you see a bat in any embroidered piece, it is likely to represent happiness, because

bat, (蝠, fú) is a homophone of fortune(福). See? They're not just blood-sucking little devils after all...!

Likewise a deer represents fame and social status, because deer, pronounced lù 鹿 is a homophone of 祿, which means something like having an imperial income.

The good ole' rooster, jī 鸡, represents luck, because you guessed it, it's a homophone of luck (吉, jí).

Furthermore, Chinese culture is one that places special emphasis on themes of auspiciousness, fortune, and luck. The essence of this aspect of Chinese culture is divided into six parts; three of which we have just looked at (fú, lù, and jí). The remaining three are Shòu (寿), which means longevity, Xǐ (喜), meaning h a p p i n e s s, and Cái (财), meaning riches or fortune. These six auspicious themes will be discussed in further detail throughout this chapter. Because of the emphasis placed on

A feast of good fortune: The character '福' with a dragon and a phoenix embroidered on it for extra auspiciousness.

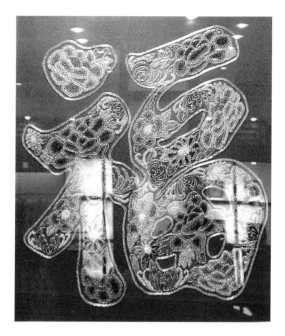

◆ *Hanging around: "福" on your wall encourages prosperity in your home.*

auspiciousness, you will find that many of the embroidered pieces you may be interested in will have special meaning related to these themes.

There are many more symbols to look out for when embroidery shopping, most based on metaphors derived from Chinese proverbs. Things that you might see include: peaches — represent longevity, peony — riches and honor, pomegranates — many sons (especially important to traditional Chinese),

sheep — filial respect, and the "eight immortals" as congratulating an elderly person on their birthday.

Incidentally, these meaning are not restricted to embroidery. If you see a painting, sculpture, or other work of art that catches your attention, the symbolism remains the same.

Now that you have some background of the symbolism found in Chinese embroidery, we can take a look at some specific examples.

Use Classic Embroidery Patterns

Understanding the metaphors of a work of art can make a world of difference in helping you decide whether you want it or not. It can also make you feel well-informed when you explain it to your friends and family. Here are nine of the best.

Longevity above Five Fu (五福捧寿)

Remember I said that bats represented fortune? Here's an example...

During the Ming and Qing dynasties, which covered a large part of the last thousand years, there was a very popular painting known as "Longevity Above Five Fu." This painting had the character for Shou (寿) circled by five flying bats.

As we know, Fu means good fortune, but through the ages there has been much debate over how to exactly define fortune. One historical record has said that the five Fu in life are longevity, wealth, peace, virtue, and a peaceful, pain-free death. In order to reach the ultimate meaning of Fu, all criteria must be attained. Although longevity is considered to be the most important, one without the others is an incomplete expression of the true meaning.

◆ *Too good to be true: The five fortunes.*

Flying fish: A carp jumps over the dragon gate.

A Carp Jumps Over Dragon Gate
（鲤鱼跃龙门）

Chinese culture reveres books and study to a very high level. In fact, books and study are so closely intertwined that common expressions for studying is dú shū 读书 (literally, "read books") and teaching is jiāo shū 教书, which literally means "to teach books." Ancient Chinese proverbs further reiterate this respect for book learning; "beauty is in the books, as is a golden existence," meaning that studying will ensure a successful, wealth generating career. The great man Confucius, bedrock of Chinese philosophical thought for millennia, said, "Study hard, lù is in it."

If studying books has always been seen as the way to gain knowledge, then exams have been seen as the way to prove it. From the mid-Tang dynasty onward, examinations were the way to win coveted places in the bureaucratic service. Generations of young Chinese scholars took these exams with utmost sincerity, and even today an echo of these past practices can be witnessed in the respect that the Chinese have for learning and education. Scholars had royal income, status, brought honor to their ancestors, and generally led luxurious lives. All the ingredients you could ask for in order to get some serious corruption happening!

This is the backdrop against which "A Carp Jumps Over Dragon Gate" needs to be looked at. This wonderfully metaphoric work of art is an expression of the massive change in fortune one would experience upon beginning the life of a government official. If the carp, an ordinary animal, can jump over the gate, it will become a dragon. The gates represent the Imperial Exams.

According to a text on written Chinese, known as Explanation of Chinese Characters, lù evolved from the character fú (福). In a sense, fú and lù have complementary meanings. To gain a title was thought of as fú, whereas to gain the favor of the king was thought of as lù.

However, within a feudal society, merit did not always remain the deciding factor. Scholars could obtain inheritable positions, thus ensuring that their offspring would be able to continue their decadent lifestyle. Many paintings, and as a result embroidered works, play on this theme. Some to look out for are "King's Teacher and Prince's Teacher," "Five sons pass the exam," "Dragon Teaches Sons," and "Nobles of Many Generations."

Remember that due to its homophonic properties, lù is often represented by a deer.

◆ *Fan-shape peony embroidery. (Photographed in White Peacock Art World). Peony was a favorite decoration in the homes of high-ranking scholars because it represents nobility and richness. This is in accordance with the social and economic status of 'carp turned dragon' scholars.*

◆ *Woolly fortune: Three sheep bring luck.*

Three Sheep
(三羊开泰)

Do you feel lucky? If you're not, then chances are you'll be looking for a piece that will invite luck (吉, jí) into your house.

One such design is that of three sheep. Sheep may be considered an odd choice for a luck-inviting animal. They smell, they're slow, and they do whatever the flock does. On the other hand, they are patient, never compete for food, and want nothing. A Chinese idiom says sān yáng kāi tài (三羊开泰), or "three sheep welcome luck." Although you may think this is an odorous and somewhat unpleasant way of inviting luck into your life, the reason for the Chinese to believe three sheep are auspicious lies once again in a brilliant pun in the Chinese language.

sān yáng, (三羊) or three sheep, is in Chinese a homophone of sān yáng (三阳), which means three male elements. Traditionally, summer in Chinese culture is associated with the masculine, and the three male elements signify the coming of summer, which is a certain and auspicious happening after the depths of winter.

So, are you feeling the warmth of summer? Grab yourself three sheep!

Eight Immortals Crossing the Sea
（八仙过海）

Eight (八, bā) is considered a lucky number in China, because it sounds like the word for prosperity fā (发). That is why the Beijing Olympics begin on the auspicious 8/8/2008 at 08:08:08 P.M. If you ever buy a cell phone in China, numbers that have multiple eights attract a higher price! In fact, the spectacular telephone number 8888-88888 sold for USD $270,723 in Chéngdū, the capital of Sìchuān!

It is therefore quite logical for the number eights to be used in many pieces of art. A theme seen time and time again is that of the Eight Immortals. In keeping with their auspicious team number, the Eight Immortals are gods who encourage people to do good things and come to the aid of those in danger or distress. Thus there are many commonly themed pieces of art, such as "The Eight Immortals Celebrating Birthday" and "The Eight Immortals Crossing the Sea."

Today, both of these are considered to have themes related to

◆ *A four-hand fairy. Invites peace and luck. (Photographed in Zitange of Gongmei Building).*

shou, or longevity. However, originally, they did not.

Deep in the mists of time, the people believed that immortal fairies lived in the mountains across the sea. Once, a fairy god invited the Eight Immortals to cross the sea for a peony-appreciating party. The gods partied long, but on the way back, they were waylaid by the Dragon King of the East Sea. After a furious battle, the Eight Immortals emerged victorious by virtue of their talismans.

Fairy worship reached new heights during the reign of China's first emperor, Qin Shihuang, (259 B.C.–210 B.C.). In a desperate bid to acquire the elixir of eternal life that the fairies held in their high mountain homes, he sent a ship with a doctor and 500 virgins across the East Sea.

Shou, you may remember, is the aspect of longevity. In later times, Shou came to be represented by fairies, because fairies never die. The Chinese believed that Old Man Fairy of the North Pole is responsible for the time people are allowed to live. This, I think, is a magical power better than that of Santa Claus.

◆ *Lucky numbers: Eight immortals crossing the sea.*

Married bliss: Double happiness.

Double Happiness
（双喜临门）

Have you ever been to a hippy hangout? Better still, did you visit Woodstock? The Tang Dynasty was Imperial China's version of the hippy culture, so it's appropriate that the pattern known as "double happiness" comes from this period. It is also the dynasty famed for the incredibly output of its poets, which also has a connection to this story.

According to stories of the past, once was a young scholar, who was traveling to the capital city to attend the final imperial exam, from which the top

scorers would enter the public service. However, on his way, in a high mountain village he was struck with illness. Luckily, he was looked after by a herbal doctor and his daughter, who nursed him back to health. In the process, he fell in love with the doctor's daughter, and she with him. As a symbol of her love, she wrote him a couplet:

Green trees against the sky in the spring rain, The sky sets off the spring trees despite their obscurity.

According to the story, she asked him to reply to her couplet. "Well," said the young man, "I need time to think it over.

I'll give you a reply after the examination." The girl nodded and gave him a mysterious smile.

Some time later, the young man arrived in the capital. Due to his diligence and intelligence, he was one of the few top-scoring students, and he won the honor of being interviewed by the emperor. However, the emperor was known to ask notoriously complicated questions. The man waited nervously for the emperor's question. It was another couplet.

***Red flowers dot the land in the chase of the breeze
The land is colored red after the kiss.***

The young man was amazed. Somehow the daughter of the doctor had given him the perfect answer to the emperor's couplet. He replied without hesitation, both startling and delighting the emperor. So impressed was he that he made the young an important minister of the empire and allowed him to travel back to his homeland before he began his work. The young man went back to his lady love and told her the news. The father, who was almost as excited as the young couple, arranged a marriage ceremony for them. As two happy events xǐ shì (喜事), in Chinese, came together, they decided to double the character xǐ (喜) for happiness, on a red piece of paper and put it on the wall.

The "double happiness" character is often used by young couples. It is found surrounded by dragons, phoenixes, or other auspicious creatures.

◆ *Magpie perched in plum tree: A homophone of happiness (by Zaihong)*

◆ *Inviting fortune: Boy, lotus, and gold fish.*

Boy, Lotus, and Gold Fish
（连年有余）

I had earlier mentioned that Chinese is a language that uses homophones to spectacular effect. Remember? I hope so, because the best example of this yet is the famous picture of the Boy, Lotus, and Gold Fish.

Fish, which is pronounced yú, (鱼) has the same pronunciation as余, which means surplus. Even better, lotus, (莲, lián) has the same pronunciation as 连 in 连年有余 lián nián yǒu yú — a Chinese saying literally meaning "surplus year after year." Chinese tradition holds that displaying such auspicious symbols, even if they are based on abstract homophonic puns, will invite good fortune into the household. And good fortune is always welcome!

In fact, good fortune, (cái in Chinese) especially in terms of money, commodities, harvests, and enterprise is taken very seriously in Chinese culture. In an ancient tome, Records of the Historian: a scholar named Sima Qian says, "You come and he comes, everyone comes for fortune, you go and he goes, everyone goes for fortune." To him the desire to obtain fortune is a social norm; it meets the law of the social development for humans to pursue their personal interests and to satisfy themselves to the fullest.

Another Chinese saying holds that, "Humans live for fortune; birds live for food." At New Year, the most common expression of celebration is not wishing you a Happy New Year, as it is in the west, but a Prosperous New Year Gōng Xǐ Fā Cái.

The culture of seeking fortune runs very deep in the Chinese psyche. So deep, in fact, that it has even penetrated religion. Traditionally the Chinese have worshipped a number of different gods to seek good fortune in their different types of work.

However, it must be remembered that although wealth is a component of fortune, it is not a blind struggle for money. Greed was looked down upon in ancient times. This may seem a contradiction in terms, but in essence the passion for good fortune should be fueled by hard work and integrity, rather than simply greed. Because of this, losing money may somewhat perversely have been seen as gaining virtue. In this way, everyone's a winner! Furthermore, seeking fortune means different things for different people. For farmers, it of course means a more prosperous harvest; to feudal officials, promotions through the bureaucratic ranks; for traders and business people, increased wealth. Some more symbols of Cái, or good fortune, are the Golden Frog, the fairy Liu Hai, and peony.

These six patterns have hopefully further introduced to you the six auspicious themes of fú (福), lù (禄), jí (吉), shòu (寿), xǐ (喜), cái (财). However, these are not the only themes you are likely to come across in embroidery in China. The following are some fun works with different auspicious symbolism.

Money matters: This embroidered fish invites a household surplus. (Photographed in White Peacock Art World)

Meeting of the giants: Dragon and phoenix.

Dragon and Phoenix
（龙凤呈祥）

We all assume that dragons are evil, right? Wrong! Unlike in Europe, here dragons were not considered to be evil in any way. The dragon represented the power of the emperor, but more than that, represented qualities of high virtue, rare talent, water, and clouds. In Chinese, the character for the dragon is 龙, pronounced "lóng."

The origins of the dragon are mysterious, however it is said that the first emperor, in a somewhat confused attempt to create a new national identity, took the totem animal of each tribe he conquered and with a little imagination came up with the dragon. Consider his unusual attributes — the body of a snake, the scales of a fish, the antlers of a stag, the face of a camel (nope, can't see that one either), the ears of a bull, the talons of an eagle, feet of a tiger, and the eyes of a demon.

Perhaps due to the origins of this unique creature as a uniting symbol of the first Chinese nation,

Han Chinese have claimed to be descendants of the dragon.

The phoenix is another of those mysterious beasts who peer at us through the half-light of time. This admirable character carries the seed of eternal truth, and is also immortal. Long ago, the male phoenix was called 凤 (fèng) and the female was called 凰 (huáng). This was thought to symbolize the harmony of Yīn and Yáng. However, today the phoenix is often simply called 凤凰 (fènghuáng). It is thought to have feminine attributes that compliment the dragon's male qualities. Together they are an unusual symbol of happiness and married bliss and are often seen hanging out together in decorations, embroidery, and paintings especially during Chinese New Year.

Two Yuanyang Ducks Playing in Water (鸳鸯戏水)

What is it about birds being associated with love? And what is it about love stories and tragedy? More than 2,000 years ago, a petty official retired to his hometown, where he decided to spend the rest of his days cultivating a beautiful garden. However, being a man of rank, he employed a gardener named Yuān to do the work for him.

One day while Yuan was toiling away in the sun he heard a scream come from the lotus pond. Turning around, he saw the daughter of the official struggling desperately in the water. In an instant, Yuan jumped into the pond and

Rising from the ashes: An embroidered phoenix from Hebei province. (Photographed in White Peacock Art World)

62

dragged her to safety. However, unknown to him, the official had also heard the scream. He ran to the garden and saw his gardener embracing his daughter. Furious, he threw Yuan into prison.

But his daughter, Yang never forgot about Yuan, the gardener. One night she secretly left home with a gift of colorful, warm clothes for her beloved gardener. It was a fatal mistake. Her father found out about the secret visit and his rage knew no bound. Despite her hysterical pleadings to spare her beloved, the official beat Yuan, tied heavy stones to his body, and had him thrown into the pond. His daughter, blinded by her pain, followed him and also drowned.

The next morning, two ducks appeared in the pond. One of them, the male, had resplendently colorful feathers, while the female was relatively plain. They swam, flew, ate, and slept together.

Even today, people look at these two ducks as symbols of long-lasting love and a happy marriage. This embroidered pattern can often be found on quilts and pillows of newly married couples.

Together forever: Two Yuanyang ducks playing in a pond.

◆ *Flaming fantastic: Kylin sending the son.*

Kylin Sending the Son
（麒麟送子）

There are four main characters in the Chinese pantheon of mythological creatures: the phoenix, dragon, tortoise, and the kylin. These creatures all share similarly auspicious characters. So it is only natural that one of them, the kylin, should make an appearance. As fantastic as the dragon, and almost as auspicious, the kylin had the hooves of an ox, the head of a dragon, horns, and often has flames all over its body, just for good measure. However, like the dragon, its fierce appearance belies its gentle nature; the kylin is a vegetarian and only punishes the wicked. Furthermore, it makes an appearance at the birth of a sage.

It is said that the day before the birth of Kongzi (孔子), Confucius in English, a kylin visited the family garden and left a gift of a jade book. The book was a symbol that foretold the fate of Confucius, which turned out to be remarkably accurate — Confucius would be extremely talented, would attain a respected rank, would be a great scholar, but was not born at the right time. Indeed, despite his latter status as the preeminent philosophical mind of China, in his lifetime Confucius was not wildly popular.

In later times, Chinese folk belief held that if you wanted a baby boy, you should obtain a painting of a little boy riding a kylin with a lotus flower in his hand. Nowadays it merely means that one wants to have a baby.

Sharp Eyes

Are you looking for antiques or something new? An investment or something as a gift for a friend? Something in the hundreds of kuai or something in the hundreds of thousands?

Assessing quality can be a tricky business. Whether it be a used car or a spouse, the true quality of your choice is not likely to become apparent until after a few years when the fabric begins to unravel and the colors begin to fade. The difference in quality, age, and cultural significance mean that the price range is vast, and so is the margin for error.

A high-quality work means a combination of excellent technique and aesthetic value. Therefore, you should pay attention to the whole composition of the picture. Technique that is not pleasing to the eye or something beautiful made quickly and carelessly, is useless.

Quality Detection

I'm assuming that you are attracted to a particular design before you start checking the technique. However, if you want to make your purchase then assessing the technique is critical for bargaining and investment purposes. I am sure you do not want to fall in love with a certain design only to have it fall to pieces in a few years. This is equally true if you want to give a precious and long-lasting gift to somebody special. To make sure they don't think your gift cheap, it is a good idea to develop some quality detection skills.

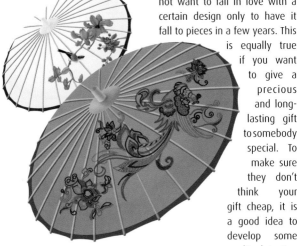

◆ *Quality detection: If it's seen through, the quality is lacking.*

Points to note

Surface:

If the surface is smooth, shining, usually the quality is good. Otherwise, if you can see the thrums or the clews, quality is probably lacking.

Thickness of the thread:

Thickness of the thread should be suited to the type of object being embroidered. A cat, for example, should be stitched with fine thread, in order to make its body feel soft and sleek like a real cat. Thick thread will make its fur feel like steel needles.

◆ *Jackpot: A high quality Oscar flower work. (by Goulswon)*

Pattern:

Something to watch out for is embroidering over a pattern that has been printed onto the fabric. If so, it is often easy to see the pattern that has been copied onto the fabric in areas where the stitching is not dense enough. As time goes by, the pattern will fade and your once gorgeous piece of art will be noticeably missing parts.

A quality piece of embroidery will have the underlying picture drawn by hand. The stitches will be dense enough to cover the entire picture.

Colors:

The colors in a piece of art are of utmost importance. Consider the subtle shades in the shadow of a tree or the eye of a cat. To attain a natural effect, there must be a large variety of colors used. For an eye, there may be more than 20 different colored threads used.

◆ *Natural effects: Embroidered lotus flower. (by Guanzhe)*

Frame:

If you are looking for embroidery purely as a form of decorative art, then the frame it comes with is also important. A quality frame is usually made of rosewood and inlaid with a traditional pattern. A cheaper one is made of coarse, tough, white wood, and will not last as long.

These tips are especially relevant if you are looking at a traditional Han piece, such as one of the "Big Four" embroidery styles of the Han Chinese. However, if it is embroidery work of another Chinese ethnic group such as the Miao, then they are not as relevant.

Remember also that the measure of a truly high-quality piece of embroidery is how much value you get out of it yourself. If you are particularly entranced by a particular pattern, then it really is an invaluable possession.

Formulating the frame: A quality work should come with a quality frame.

Hand vs Machine: Spotting the difference

In ancient times...no, just kidding, this is not another one of those "in ancient times" stories! China, as you may have noticed, (how could you not?) is the factory of the world. One thing made in China is sewing machines. They are manufactured in the millions.

Not only is the sewing machine industry booming, but also the machine-made embroidery industry. This makes it more difficult for handmade pieces

Brilliant blossom: A handmade embroidery peony. (Photographed in White Peacock Art World)

to compete, and has the added side effect of inspiring fewer young people to learn the art.

Furthermore, the quality of machine-made pieces continues to improve, leading some dishonest vendors to try and pass off machine-made pieces as genuine handmade ones.

Thankfully, spotting the difference between hand and machine-made embroidery is a pretty easy skill to master if you want to buy silk embroidery. The easiest and most obvious thing

What to look out for: This is an example of machine-made flowers.

to know is that you cannot make silk embroidery with a machine. Silk is too brittle to be stitched with a powerful machine and will break too easily. Machine stitched embroidery therefore is most often made with nylon, which is more shiny and fine.

Another thing to check is the back of the piece. The fabric of a handmade piece is not going to have the military uniformity of a machine-stitched one.

The overwhelming majority of such classics as "Four Seasons" and "Plum, Orchid, Bamboo, and Chrysanthemum" in China's embroidery market are machine made. However, hand-stitched versions can still be found if you are willing to look for them. Just be careful that if you are paying for a hand-stitched one you are indeed getting a hand-stitched one!

Certificates

◆ *Prestigious prizes: The Golden Blossom Flower Cup Award.*
(Provided by Zaihong)

A certificate is a guarantee that what you have is the real McCoy and therefore worthy of collecting. Masters of the art use certificates to ensure their good name is recognized. A standard certificate should include an introduction of the embroiderer including their name, gender, a photo, and their title.

Respect for learning and achieving specialized knowledge runs very deep in Chinese culture, as does a long history of bureaucracy. It should come as no surprise, then,

Confirmation of quality: The professional certificate of arts and crafts. (Provided by Zaihong)

that practitioners of different forms of the arts obtain formal recognition through standardized levels of skill. There are four main levels of recognition: the Art worker, Assistant Art & Craft Technologist, Art & Craft Technologist, and Master of Art.

Only pieces made by people in the two top levels are valuable to collect. Some really famous Masters of Art are Madame Jiang Zaihong and Mr. Su Huo. Madame Jiang has won the highest honor in the field of Chinese embroidery — the Golden Blossom Flower Cup. Her piece was called "Roaring Lion." Mr. Su also won the same award, interestingly, for an embroidered portrait of former UN General Secretary Kofi Annan.

Next is an introduction of the piece itself including a picture,

an explanation of the metaphors and symbolism in the piece, the techniques used, and the time spent working on it.

Like great painted art, a high-quality embroidered work is considered exceptional not just because of its brilliant use of technique, but also the deeper themes expressed in the picture. If the metaphorical value of the piece is weak or tired, the piece will not fetch a good price, especially in a nation as obsessed with auspiciousness as China.

In order to help you determine how rare or otherwise the piece is, the certificate should also include how many similar-themed pieces the embroiderer had made. It is important to note that embroidered art is not like teapots, which can be produced in the hundreds. A really good quality piece is likely to be the only one in existence.

If there is more than one of the same piece in existence, a serial number should be included.

Due to the labor-intensive nature of the work, large embroidered pieces are often the result of collaboration between several people. In this case the name of the company may be written on the certificate, rather than the individual names of all the workers.

Remember, only the cream of embroidered art has certificates. Asking for some sort of verification for the piece that cost you a few hundred yuan is futile.

◆ *Example of excellence: A certificate of art. (Provided by Chen Zaifang)*

Keep an eagle eye on "Ancient Pieces"

Many an unwary traveler has come to the Middle Kingdom in search of treasure and left with a cheap piece they spent a fortune on. If you are not an expert, it is best not to pretend.

One of the most common tricks that you may encounter is people by the roadside selling small clay or bronze figures they

claim to have dug up from a tombs or that their ancestors left them. Often people get taken in by it. Don't be fooled!

Beware of the hard sell. Some visitors have felt pressured into buying things they haven't had the time to check properly. It's a good idea to ask yourself the three "Ws" in situations where you are not sure. The first is "why." If you are in a market where every store seems to be loaded with valuable artifacts, you should be asking yourself why there are so many valuable items left. The second is "where." Are you at a place recognized for its quality of authentic goods? The last one is "who." Who made this piece? Are you sure it was who they claim it was? Have you seen other pieces made by the same person? Remember, if you lack the historical and cultural knowledge needed to discern fake from genuine, it is better not to take too many risks.

Auctions are one of the few places where you can be fairly sure that what you will buy is what it is supposed to be, because it should have had its quality appraised in advance. However, the downfall is that you will have a lot of competition.

Luckily for you, there are several auction houses whose main business is valuable antique art, including antique embroidery. China Guardian Auction Co. Ltd (http://www.cguardian.com) is one such business. Established in 1993, it specializes in Chinese art of all varieties and holds major international spring and fall auctions, as well as smaller, seasonal auctions. You can check out their Web site for more information on time, places, and bidding processes. If you are really interested, it also provides information regarding laws on auctions and the protection of cultural relics. Beijing Hanhai Auction Co. Ltd (http://www.hanhai.net) is another good choice. This company was established in 1994 and its main business is similar to that of China Guardian Auctions. In the past few years, it has become more and more highly regarded for auctioning antique

◆ *Timeless: An antique Miao work. (Photographed in Pan Yuzhen's home)*

◆ *East and West: The embroidered portrait of the Mona Lisa (Provided by Goulswon). In an April 2007 Beijing auction it was sold for RMB 5.5 million.*

embroidery. In November 2005, it sold a piece called "Fairies Celebrating a Birthday" for RMB 418,000, or US $59,000.

If embroidered fans are where your interest lies, check out these few companies. They may not have their entire sites translated into English, so you may need some assistance in reading them:

Emperor's Ferry International Auction Co., ltd
(http://www.chinaefa.com);

Beijing Rongbao Auctions Co., ltd
(http://www.art139.com);

Pacific International Auction Co., ltd
(http://www.piac.com.cn)

ZhongHongXin International Auction Co., ltd
(http://www.zhxpm.com)

International Auction Co. of China
(http://www.china-auction.cn)

Christie's
(http://www.christies.com)

Before an auction begins there is normally an exhibition of the pieces. You visit an exhibition, study each piece carefully, and think about how much you might want to spend on a given piece. If you have a friend who has sufficient knowledge on such matters it is a good idea to take him or her along. Also check out if the piece you are interested in

◆ *Elegant choice: Antique Miao embroidery used to carry children on one's back. (Photographed in Pan Yuzhen's home)*

budget. Remember to stay cool under the pressure of the moment and not to do anything silly such as mortgage your house for the sake of a piece of art!

The more you are willing to spend on a piece, the more careful you should be that it is indeed a worthwhile investment. As such, online auctions should be handled with care. If you are looking at something that is claimed to be an antique online, it is necessary to get independent verification, from a third party, if possible.

comes with a certificate.

Remember it is not a good idea to set your heart on only one piece, if you can help it. If this happens and that piece ends up being sold for too much money, then you will not have any second options.

On the day of the auction, just play the casual observer when the piece you like first appears. This is a good way to assess the level of interest in your piece and also may give an early indication if it is going to go for a price far beyond your

Reference
Price

Feel like investing, but not sure how to go about it? The good news is that you can make worthwhile returns on the right piece of embroidery.

The Market

Over recent years, quality embroidery, especially vintage pieces, have experienced a surge in prices, as more international people have become aware of the art form and the performance of the economy has allowed more Chinese people to spend their income on luxury items.

In fact, in the past several years the cost of verified, quality antique pieces has risen by as many as 10 times. In the 2004 Spring Han Hai Auction, a piece named "Eighteen Arhats" sold for 19,800 RMB ($2,800). However, it is interesting to know that this piece came from the Yuan dynasty, and was made by Guan Zhongji, who was the wife of a great painter. It is thus quite a priceless, cultural artifact in its own right. Even more incredible, it was originally expected to fetch 3,000 RMB ($400).

This is good news for the collector, as not only will you be investing in an aesthetically pleasing work of art, but also something that will give you a good return on your money. Today, pieces from the Ming and Qing dynasties are fetching prices up to 300,000 RMB!

However, age does not necessarily make a piece a wise

◆ *Dapper duds: A traditional Miao summer top. (Photographed in Pan Yuzhen's home)*

◆ *Stunning sleeves: There is often a lot of detail in Miao embroidery.*
(Photographed in Pan Yuzhen's home)

investment. Some older pieces suffer from faded colors, and others may not attract good prices simply because they are visually appealing.

The best pieces to look for in terms of investment return are those that have distinct local features. The pieces are carriers of folklore and history, and will no doubt rise in price considerably as people become more aware of their cultural significance.

◆ *Quirky and quixotic: Traditional Miao shoes.*
(Photographed in Pan Yuzhen's home)

Sublime head gear: An old Miao hat for children, front side. (Photographed in Pan Yuzhen's home)

collection of embroidered 3-inch shoes. This is not a joke. You may be aware of the former practice of binding girl's feet so they would not properly grow. This was considered highly attractive. There are still some of these shoes made for personal collections, although the practice has long since died out.

At the end of the day, however, you must ask yourself what you want to collect. Being aware of what you are after is a must before you start loading your suitcases with pieces that in a few years you will not appreciate anymore. You don't want your house to become a warehouse of random, useless embroidery.

How about a collection of tigers for your living room wall? That would spice up an evening with your guests....

An interesting approach is to collect pieces based on one theme. There are some famous personal collections in China that have been developed in this way. Shanghai resident Bao Wanhua, for example, collects embroidered opera dresses. An American couple has an excellent

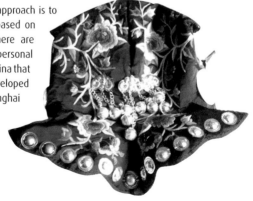

Reverse view: From the back side. (Photographed in Pan Yuzhen's home)

Price Calculator

The price of a piece of embroidery depends on many factors. These include the type and quality of fabrics, thread, the frame, and the time involved, to say nothing of its age or the status of the embroiderer. However, of these factors, the labor of a handmade piece will account for about 85 percent of the overall cost. This is why a handmade piece is so much more expensive than a machine-made one.

In addition, there are some other general rules that apply to assessing the true cost of a piece of embroidery. Check out the calculator below......

Calculating Hint No. 1

Factor 1: Patterns

Price rule: portrait and human figure embroidery > scenery and woods one> still life and oil painting one> landscape painting one> animal one> traditional flowers and plants one

Explanation: People who have the skills to embroider human figures are very rare, because they need to be talented and experienced in fine arts, as well as embroidery. Landscapes, still lifes and oil paintings are normally done by skilled young people. However, many people master the comparatively simpler skill of embroidering traditional depictions of flowers and plants.

◆ *A Western twist: This kind of still life is usually more expensive than similar traditional Chinese patterns. (Photographed in White Peacock Art World)*

Factor 2: Embroidery Methods

Price rule: double-sided embroidery> single-sided one

Explanation: It's simple, really. Single-sided embroidery is far simpler than double-sided one. The technique involved in double-sided embroidery is quite complex, and this raises the labor cost to about one and a half times that of its single-sided counterpart.

Factor 3: Colors

Price rule: rich, vivid-color embroidery>less, light-color one

Explanation: The richer and more vivid the colors, the more different color thread used. This will mean that during the process of embroidery, the person must change needles and threads quite frequently. This extends the process and drives the labor cost higher. However, it also drives the aesthetic quality up.

◆ *Ethereal insects: This is a double-sided butterfly embroidery piece. Double-sided pieces are usually more expensive than single-sided. (Photographed in White Peacock Art World)*

The Scroll of the Song Dynasty. The big one is RMB 21,000.00, and the small one is RMB 8,500.00. (Photographed in White Peacock Art World)

Factor 4: Size

Price rule: big-size embroidery> small-size one

Explanation: Size does count... a bit. Naturally, there is often more work in a bigger piece of embroidered art than a smaller one.

Factor 5: Stitch

Price rule: dense, short stitches> sparse, long stitches

Explanation: Once again, dense stitches take more time and effort, driving up the labor cost.

Earthly paradise: A view of Jiuzhaigou, Sichuan Province. (Provided by Goulswon) Usually the rich, vividly colored embroidery is more expensive than the less vivid and lighter-colored one.

Factor 6: Thread

Price rule: split-threads embroidery > non-split one

Explanation: Split threads add visual excitement to a piece of embroidery. Furthermore, thinner threads and shorter needles require a lot of patience and very good eyesight!

A quality piece of embroidery may require four times as many hours than the same piece of a much lesser quality. As such, there can be a significant difference in price according to the quality! However, quality pieces of embroidery are culturally priceless works of art, and worth every cent, penny, or yuan you choose to spend on them.

Sample Embroidery Art Pieces

Sample 1 Bamboo （檀木竹子）

Category: double-sided
*Size: 50cm * 25 cm*
Reference Price: RMB36,000.00

"I can live without meat, but I cannot live without bamboo. No meat makes people slim, no bamboo makes people insincere and artificial. Slim people can put on weight again, but insincerity and artificiality cannot be rooted out."

That, my friends, is how serious the Chinese have traditionally

◆ *Beautiful bamboo art*

taken the role of bamboo in their culture. The quote is from a famous Song Dynasty poet, Su Dongpo. A little over the top, you may think, but reverence for bamboo is incredibly strong in historical Chinese sources.

The secret to a great artistic depiction of bamboo lies in its delicate subtlety. The bamboo looks simple to paint, but takes a lifetime to master. Age, light, and millions of natural variations between plants make it a quixotically mysterious subject to know with the deft skills of an accomplished artist. Those aspiring to paint or embroider it in all its glory often keep plants at home in order to become more and more familiar with it over a long period of time.

Thus what looks like a deceivingly simple, if elegant, double-sided embroidered work of bamboo above is actually an extremely complex work of understated brilliance. Through the picture, one can gain a sense of graceful suppleness and honesty of the plant. The aesthetic value of the work is simple to observe. But are the metaphors in the piece also as dazzling?

Bamboo is a constant theme in Chinese arts, be it in paintings, poems, metaphorical allusions, or embroidery. Bamboo is firm, upright, divided into segments, and hollow inside. In the grand tradition of the Chinese penchant for homophones, in the past these qualities have been linked to moral virtues of inner strength, trustworthiness, modesty, and openness. In the cold winter weather, the bamboo still remains strong and green despite the fact that other plants wither and die. Such a quality is considered very admirable in Chinese culture.

These fine virtues dovetail into the characteristics that the Chinese find admirable in men of virtue, and especially of religious virtue. In Taoist and Buddhist tradition, many holy men were hermits who spent their lives wrapped in the solitude of nature. Being surrounded by bamboo was considered highly conducive to a monk leading a pious life devoid of earthly concerns, as can be seen in the quote above.

Another one of these holy hermits, Wang Wei, the famous poet of the Tang Dynasty who is known as the Buddha Poet, touchingly described his ideal life as "sitting alone among the bamboo, playing an instrument and singing, with only the moon for company."

So synonymous did bamboo become with virtue over time that scholars of high standing and integrity became known as jūnzǐ 君子 — literally bamboo. This can be said to be the highest form of compliment.

Allow the bamboo to ensure you never become insincere or artificial....

Sample 2 Eight Horses (八骏图)

Category: double-sided
*Size: 50cm * 30cm*
Reference Price: RMB 7,300.00

A horse is a horse, of course. But a horse is also the source of a whole lot of force. The seventh animal in the Chinese zodiac is an apt physical representation of power, strength, perseverance, and prosperity. A group of eight horses like the one below is also representative of the herd owned by King Mu during the 10th century. This kind of depiction is a symbol of growth and fortune in terms of business.

The idiom at the top right corner of this exhilarating work, which says "mǎ dào chéng gōng," 马 到成功 is also reflective of these

Horsing around: A traditional symbol of fortune and strength.

◆ *Excitable equines: Can you imagine an army of Mongol warriors bearing down on you from these horsebacks?*

themes. The first character, mǎ means horse; the second, dào means something like bring or send; and the last two, chéng gōng, mean success or achievement. Thus "horses bring success" is surely a great addition to your office wall or as a symbolic gift to somebody about to enter a testing period.

Looking at the piece, one can sense the freedom of the herd galloping across the Mongolian steppe without care in the world or an obstacle in their path. Harnessing this kind of positive energy is a plus in many ventures.

Sample 3 Carp and Lotus (鲤鱼戏莲)

Category: double-sided
Size: diameter = 35cm
Reference Price: RMB 2,000.00

We have already discussed the marvelous metaphors behind the work Carp, Lotus, and Boy in Chapter 2. But what are the metaphors behind Carp and Lotus? If it were simple, it would not be a part of the culture of China.

The lotus is a magnificent plant steeped in magical metaphor. It is born and grows in muck, but it manages to maintain its own splendor and stays untouched by muck itself. Thus it is seen as incorruptible and therefore symbolizes chastity and nobility.

Encouragingly for those who wish to bear children, it also produces a lot of seeds. Even better, in Chinese the word for seed is a homophone of son, or baby.

Furthermore, a lover's relationship is often likened to that of the relationship between fish and water. The Carp and Lotus pattern is therefore highly symbolic for harmonious relationships of couples and the wish to have more children.

◆ *Carp and Lotus: A magnificent metaphor.*

Sample 4 Blossom Peony （花开富贵）

Category: double-sided
Size: diameter = 35cm
Reference Price: RMB 3,800.00

The peony is known as "The Flower of Riches and Honor" in Chinese, a name that is definitely worthy of the gorgeous flower depicted above. It is a symbol of feminine beauty and an emblem of love and affection.

Over time many other titles have been bestowed upon this fortuitous flower, including "The Queen of a Hundred Flowers," "The Flower with the Noble Character," and "The Flower of the Heavenly Scent."

The fragrance of peonies has been particularly celebrated over time, especially by Tang Dynasty poet, Li Zheng Feng. His particularly flowery verse described the peony as having "celestial fragrance" with the most radiant color in the country and whose fragrance permeated the countryside.

Peonies have traditionally symbolized peace, happiness, and thriving prosperity. If you feel like your life is in such a state at this point in time, then the peony is the one for you. The delicately crafted and stylish frame in which this piece sits is also highly complementary to the visual feast in front of you.

Sample 5 Flowers and Birds Folding Screen
(花鸟屏风)

Category: double-sided
*Size: 50cm * 32 cm*
Reference Price: RMB1,250.00

I think we'd all agree that sometimes less is more, and such is the case for this petite Flower and Bird folding screen.

◆ *Prosperous peony:' The flower of riches and honor.'*

Harmony, longevity, prosperity. What more could one ask for in a folding screen?

This kind of piece is perfect for decorating coffee tables, desks, or mantelpieces.

Flowers and birds have long been favored themes of artists in China — it is natural for people to interpret and represent their natural surroundings in an artistic manner. This double-sided folding screen contains three plants; bamboo, plum, and pine. Bamboo has already been discussed in detail, but plum is representative of purity and pine of moral uprightness.

For extra auspiciousness, birds have been added to the mix. The crane is a classic Chinese symbol of longevity. The yellow birds represent harmony and the golden pheasants represent a prosperous future. This piece is thus a harmonious combination of many auspicious symbols. It's so lucky that it could almost grow wings and fly away.

Sample 6 Two Yuanyang Ducks Playing in Water (鸳鸯戏水)

Category: double-sided
Size: diameter = 15 cm
Reference Price: RMB 450.00

Looking at this delicately crafted work, the tragic story behind it seems all the more poignant. See Chapter 3 for the story.

Sample 7 Carp in Duckweed (浮萍鲤鱼)

Category: Double-sided
*Size: 53cm * 50cm*
Reference Price: RMB 96,000.00

The symbolism of carp has been discussed at length elsewhere, but by itself it simply signifies great wealth. Wealthy Chinese people will often display carp in their homes. Carp are also found in ponds at many of the tourist locations you are likely to visit during your time in China, especially in the south.

The fabrics used in a masterpiece such as this are often so fine that it is translucent. Note the three-dimensional effect of the piece — the carp seems to be swimming away from you. This is a result of the use of translucent fabric.

While working on a delicate translucent fabric, the artist must display extraordinary amounts of skill and patience in order to bring the picture to

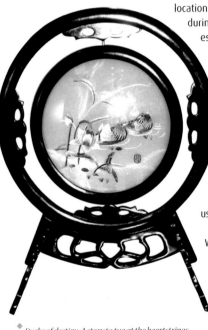

Ducks of destiny: A story to tug at the heartstrings.

life. I wish I could paint like this. Then I'd have pictures of carp on my wall too....

Crème de la carp: A fishy symbol of wealth.

The red plum blossom below is a delicately understated rendition of the plant itself. Other depictions with metaphors that is based on homophones are quite commonly seen. A famous example is that of "Happiness on the Eyebrows," which just means extremely joyful. This depicts a magpie sitting on the branch of a plum tree. In Chinese magpie sounds exactly the same as "joyful bird" and plum tree has the same pronunciation as eyebrow,

Sample 8 Plum blossom（红梅）

Category: double-sided
Size: diameter = 20cm
Reference Price: RMB 980.00

The plum blossom is one of the tougher characters in the world of flowers. Where other, more delicate specimens wither and die it soldiers on, maintaining its color and beauty.

But plum is more than that. At the dawn of spring, plum is the first blossom to greet the new season. The plum blossom is therefore an auspicious symbol welcoming spring after the harshness of winter.

Pugnacious plum blossom: A symbol of auspiciousness and a hardy survivor.

so the idiom is captured in the seemingly unrelated picture of a bird perched on a branch. The subtlety of this language never ceases to amaze!

Sample 9 Pine and Crane
（松鶴延年）

Category: double-sided
Size: diameter = 35cm
Reference Price: RMB3,800.00

After the death of a Taoist priest, he was said to be "turning into a feathered Crane." These sagacious creatures were respected for their longevity, which in traditional east Asian cultures was synonymous with wisdom.

Unlike Western culture, with its emphasis on youth, age has traditionally been held in high esteem in the East. Feng Shui beliefs hold that displaying a crane in your home will welcome wisdom into your life. After the phoenix, the crane is the most important bird in Chinese folklore and art. It has one big advantage, though, that it actually exists. However, previous beliefs that it is immortal may be somewhat overstated.

Another auspicious, but easily overlooked, metaphor in the work above is the inclusion of the pine tree on which the cranes are perched. Pines, like bamboo, are evergreen and are therefore thought to have a strong and indomitable character.

Age-old wisdom: Would the crane be a suitable company in your study?

Cranes are said to maintain a strong interest in human affairs. Can you imagine this wise crane sitting in your living room watching over all that you are doing?

◆ *Isolated orchid: The noble scholar of the flower world?*

Sample 10 Orchid
（兰花）

Category: double-sided
*Size: 25cm * 20cm*
Reference Price: RMB1,560.00

The orchid's fragrance should be enjoyed by royalty in their residence
But they look so solitary among grasses in the wild.
They are not unlike noble scholars who no one appreciates

And who have to be content with the company of common classes.

This is an interesting quote by Confucius, a man who spent many years wandering in an effort to promote his philosophies and became revered only long after his death. He spent 10 years of his life traveling around the Kingdom of Zhou in an attempt to gain a ministerial position. The position of orchid in Chinese folklore is, in fact, attributed to this unappreciated sage, who is said to have developed a special fondness for the plant in his early age.

Since the Confucian era, the orchid has been widely used in literary and artistic works. In both classic and modern literature, the plum (梅), the orchid (兰), the bamboo (竹), and the chrysanthemum (菊) are referred to as "the noble four" (四君子) plants.

Sample 11 Cat （猫）

Category: double-sided
Size: diameter = 20cm
Reference Price: RMB 980.00

This feline friend knows how to play the cuteness card. Who wouldn't want to rescue this poor pussy from his perch? The translucent fabric in the background effectively adds a sense of loneliness to this charming cat.

◆ *Crafty cat: Wouldn't you want to take this cute creature home?*

Sample 12 Leopard
(豹子)

Category: Single-sided
*Size: 40cm * 50cm*
Reference Price: RMB 14,400.00

Frightening feline: Would you dare to pass this leopard if you were up to no good?

There are no patterns in Chinese art quite as exhilarating as the big cats that prowl their paintings and embroidery with terrifying intensity. There is a good reason for their ferocious appearance — they are expected to help ward off evil spirits. Tigers especially are often used as emblems to protect houses.

Sample 13 Chinese Rose
(月季)

Category: single-sided
*Size: 40cm * 50cm*
Reference Price: RMB 7,120.00

In Western culture, the rose has long been viewed as a symbol of love, grace, and innocence, depending on its color. A red rose like the one below has been a symbol of love.

Chinese roses are also considered auspicious because they bloom all year around. If they are put in a group of four, they are thought to represent the four seasons.

As a universal symbol of love or auspiciousness, a rose like the one below would be a gorgeous addition to any living room wall.

A flower for four seasons: The romantic rose.

◆ *Thespian appeal: Even characters from French plays have become the subjects of Chinese embroidery.*

Sample 14 La Dame aux camellias (茶花女)

Category: Single-sided
*Size: 55cm * 40cm*
Reference Price: RMB 42,000.00

This distinctly non-Chinese looking lady is a character from Camille, the 19th century French play by Alexandre Dumas, fils.

Historically, portraits have been considered the most difficult aspect of embroidery to master. At this point in time, there are several active portrait masters plying their trade in China.

Professor Wei Jingxian of Wenzhou University is one of them. In 1985, his color portrait embroidery of Princess Diana was presented as a state gift to the Princess of Wales, who praised it highly for both its quality and striking resemblance. He has also embroidered Queen Elizabeth II, Mao Zedong, and Jiang Zhongzheng at the Negotiation at Chongqing, among others.

It is also possible to have a portrait of you or a loved one made.

Sample 15 Hall （门厅）

Category: single-sided
*Size: 65cm * 65cm*
Reference Price: RMB 8,500.00

Along with visual art and poetry, architecture is another jewel in the Chinese cultural crown. Examples of their skilfull use of space, incorporation of communal areas into homes, and gorgeous gardens is hard to miss if you visit any ancient buildings or si he yuan (traditional houses). This example is the view from a traditional hall thought to be in early 20th century Beijing. However it would not have looked out of place hundreds of years earlier or in many different areas all over the country. To look at this is to gain a sense of an everyday scene for millions of Chinese people over many historical generations.

A view from the East: A little Chinese history in your living room.

Sample 16 Dragon Oriental Painting Vase （龙瓶）

Category: single-sided
*Size: 68cm * 90cm*
Reference Price: RMB11,800.00

Now for something that is a little more out of the ordinary. Embroidery has drawn inspiration from many braches of the arts,

although paintings are the most common discipline from which it is derived. This particular piece is taken from a porcelain vase, wrapped by a protective dragon, which is, incidentally, the master of water. Dragons have been discussed elsewhere, but it is interesting to see in what kind of contexts they are represented in embroidered art.

◆ *Lord of water: The dragon sits very well on a vase.*

Sample 17 Four-Season Safety (四季平安)

Category: single-sided
*Size: 91cm * 111cm*
Reference Price: RMB126,000.00

Does this look familiar? It isn't quite Chinese? Lovers of art will recognize it as Van Gogh's Sunflower. If you have had a bit of an overdose of traditional Chinese patterns of auspiciousness and good fortune, you will be happy to know that there are other kinds of e m b r o i d e r y, including works by other famous E u r o p e a n painters.

In Chinese, vase is a homophone of safety. These flowers and their vase thus have the additional Chinese metaphor of representing both safety and security.

Dutch delights: Van Gogh is one of the Western artists whose paintings can be found in embroidered form.

Preservation Skills

Like a vintage car or an antique dish, embroidered art must be treated respectfully and with a lot of tender care. A real masterpiece should be treated with all the concern you would give a newborn baby.

The following guidelines are for those who invest in expensive works of art. There are four main things to remember:

Cleaning and repairing

If you, God forbid, somehow end up with a stain on your precious piece of art, then you should seek expert advice about how, or indeed, whether to repair it. It is essential to ensure that the cleaning or repairing will not harm the piece. Antique pieces can be fragile and you may just have to accept fading as part of its aging charm. Remember, never just repair it because you want some brighter colors.

Recording

Keeping good records makes sense for reselling reasons and passing it down to the next generation. You should retain information such as year, name, materials, type, maker, where and when made and bought, and anything else you have available. Also, getting a collection serial number is very important.

Storing

Embroidery is delicate. It is shy of the sun, as harsh UV rays make its fabric fade and become brittle. Moisture is also damaging to its long-term quality, but too dry an environment is equally bad. You also need to consider that the ideal storage place should not be infested with insects.

Do not fold the piece. If you store different pieces on top of one another, place thin, white paper between them.

More Miao get up: On the right side of this piece, there are some stains. If you accidentally stain an embroidered item, you should ask an expert before dealing with the problem. (Photographed in Pan Yuzhen's Home)

◆ *Antique apron: When you collect a piece, spread it out. Never fold it.*
(Photographed in Pan Yuzhen's home)

◆ *TLC is crucial: Never expose your*
embroidery collection to strong
sunlight or moisture.

Public viewing

If you would like to show your embroidered art to friends and family, you should wash and dry your hands and put on a pair of clean gloves before you touch it. Never touch it directly with your fingers, and do not let your guests stand too close to it in case moisture or germs from their breath damage it. If you want to look very closely yourself, it is best to put on a mask, or at least hold your breath.

Souvenirs and Presents

The word "souvenir" comes from the Latin root sub venir, meaning "to come to mind." A real souvenir should therefore be a memento that reminds you of the place you have visited. All too often, when in a different country, it's easy to buy something that looks great at the time but soon loses its significance when you return home.

This is where Chinese embroidery is different. If you choose the right piece, embroidery is a timeless reminder of this ancient country and its culture. Furthermore, a quality piece can survive generations, if properly cared for.

Small Filled Pieces

These small items are a traditional lover's gift. Young women would make them and fill them with soft cotton and fragrant materials, and they would give them to their beloved for good luck.

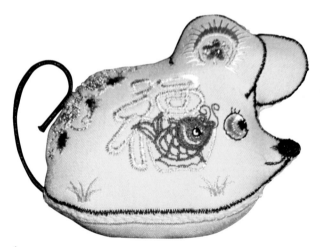

Resourceful rat: Since 2008 is the year of the Rat as well as the Olympics, many people like to buy rat-decorated things. (Photographed in Wangfujing Area)

Small bags

A handy and stylish way of carrying your knick-knacks, small bags such as these can be found with a huge variety of patterns, both Eastern and Western.

◆ *Fusion of new and old: Although embroidery is a traditional skill, the pattern can be modern. (Photographed in Jing Xiu)*

◆ *Getting lippy. Even a lipstick box can be made beautifully. (Photographed in Nanluogu Xiang)*

Box of Lipstick

These gorgeous little bags function as lipstick holders! No matter how small an embroidered item you are looking for, you can easily find it if you look hard enough.

106

Mirror

You don't need a wall to hang your mirror on when you have an attractive piece like this. Portable and stylish, this can be carried anywhere without problem.

◆ Mirror, mirror, on the wall: A small, heart-shaped mirror with embroidered back. (Photographed in Nanluogu Xiang)

Business Card Box

◆ Crafty contact cards: With a traditional Han dynasty pattern. (Photographed in Jing Xiu)

No, they are not wallets. These are cases for your business cards, which are highly valued in China. Incidentally, if you ever give or receive a card from a local Chinese person, make sure you use both hands as a sign of respect. It is considered very rude not to use both hands in this situation and may end up costing you some great business opportunities!

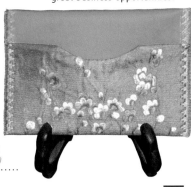

◆ Business box: With a plum blossom pattern. (Photographed in Jing Xiu)

Notebook

Who wouldn't want to keep a personal record of their life if they have a notebook of such quality? Although the art of diary writing is dying out, a gift such as this may be able to tempt an elderly loved one to commit their life's experience to paper. Or if nothing else, a quality notebook is always valued.

Embroidered words: Notebook with an embroidered dress pattern. (Photographed in Nanluogu Xiang)

Wallet

Tired of buying cheap wallets that fall to pieces after a few months? An embroidered wallet is your solution.

Caring for your cash: A row of embroidered wallets. (Photographed in Jing Xiu)

◆ *Money matters: Up close to an embroidered wallet. (Photographed in Jing Xiu)*

Cell phone Bag

These little bags bring together the modern cell phones within the wraps of the ancient art of embroidery.

A traditional twist: Two Miao-style embroidered cell phone bags. (Photographed in Wangfujing area)

Handbag

Something that knows no cultural or national boundaries is, it seems, the handbag.

◆ *Handy handbag: Something you don't often see; embroidered handbags. (Photographed in Jing Xiu)*

Shoulder Bag

Women's style bags are relatively easy to find but you can also get "manbags" if you look hard enough. Or even better, with the help of a specialist, design your own.

Small and simple: Yet this bag also manages to be attractive and functional. ◆

◆ *Nothing like the classics: An old Miao-style bag. (Photographed in Lamu)*

Cool colors: Another old Miao-style bag with a butterfly and flower pattern.
(Photographed in Lamu)

Coasters and placemats

Coasters and placemats can be found in a wide variety of Chinese and Western styles. There is another use for placemats if you do not wish to put them on your dining table — you can always hang them on the wall.

◆ *Dignified dining: Handmade coaster and placemat with Chinese goldfish and crane patterns. (Photographed in White Peacock Art World)*

◆ *Stylish accessories: Two placemats, one with a 'double happiness' pattern, other with Yuanyang ducks pattern. (Photographed in Nanluogu Xiang)*

Fit for an emperor: A round, red placemat with a yellow dragon on it. (Photographed in Wangfujing area)

An Oriental twist: Traditional Chinese handmade coaster with peony blossom patterns. (Photographed in Jing Xiu)

Desk Mat

Feeling studious? A desk mat is a study aid for the serious scholar. I would suggest going for themes that reflect intellectual industriousness.

Up close and personal: You can see the detail in this pattern. (Photographed in White Peacock Art World)

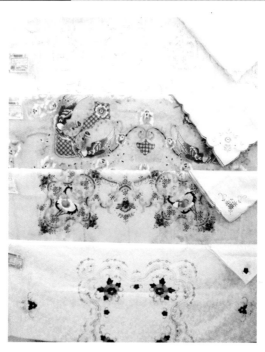

Imperial exam aid: Desk mats on sale. (Photographed in White Peacock Art World)

Chair Mat

Designed to provide a warm cushion on cold, winter days, they also look great if you choose the right pattern.

Seated comfort: A Miao-style chair mat. (Photographed in Nanluogu Xiang)

Handkerchief

A little old fashioned, perhaps, but hankies are still a lot more practical than tissues, and if nobody else, your grandmother might appreciate them.

Nose paraphernalia: A silk handkerchief. (Photographed in Wangfujing area)

Plentiful progeny: A hundred-child patterned cushion. (Photographed in Wangfujing area)

Cushion

Cushions are a great addition to many rooms in the house, including bedrooms, living rooms, and even kitchens or dining rooms if the patterns are decorative. The advantage with these pillows is that not only are they functional, they are also great to appreciate just for their looks.

Classy comfort: A row of embroidered cushions. (Photographed in Wangfujing area)

Distinctive style: A colorful Miao pattern. (Photographed in Lamu)

Pillow and Quilt Cover

If you choose a great set of pillow and quilt covers, it can make your whole room look luxurious. Would you like to have your bedroom chambers fit for an emperor?

Time to snooze: Embroidered pillow and quilt cover. (Provided by Emperor)

Waistband and Bellyband

Embroidered clothes are not just for women, but it seems that there are more items available for women. Two of such examples are waistbands and bellybands.

Old-fashioned trends: A bellyband corsage traditionally worn by Chinese women. (Photographed in Wangfujing area)

Abundant elegance: Beautiful, ethnic waistbands. (Photographed in Nanluogu Xiang)

Qipao

The Qipao is the modernized version of the clothing worn by the Manchurian founders of the Qing dynasty, who conquered China in the 17th century. Remember you can order them tailor-made.

◆ *The real deal: An embroidered Qipao next to an illustrated one.*
(Photographed in Wangfujing area)

Scarf

These scarves will make you stand out in a crowd and keep you warm.

In the store: A girl surnamed Huang shows a beautiful scarf sold in her shop. (Photographed in Nanluogu Xiang)

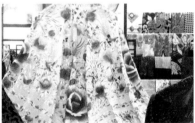

Scarfilicious: A world of embroidered scarves. (Photographed in White Peacock Art World)

Flower power: A model wearing a black scarf with red roses.

Dress

It could be said of both modern and ancient Chinese clothes that the wearer attempts to convey some kind of meaning from what they dress in, even if it is to convey "I'm feeling sleepy and don't want to work today." If you want to buy traditional, embroidered clothes, there are several ways you might like to go about it. You could focus purely on the aesthetics, or pay more attention to the metaphors. You might go for historical value, or you might just want to buy the most shocking and outrageous item you can find.

◆ *Delightful dresses: The model wears three handmade, embroidered dresses. (Photographed in Wangfujing area)*

◆ *Stunning silk: A dress of flower-patterned pure silk. (Photographed in Wangfujing area)*

Stylish, small fries: Embroidered clothes for kids. (Photographed in White Peacock Art World)

Exotic apparel: An embroidery Miao-style dress. (Photographed in Lamu)

Pajama

Although associated with the ferociousness of Bruce Lee, the dragon is a protective rather than aggressive beast.

◆ *Enter the dragon: Embroidered silk pajamas with traditional dragon pattern. (Photographed in Wangfujing area)*

◆ *More detail: A close up of the dragon. (Photographed in Wangfujing area)*

Underwear

Silk is perhaps the sexiest of underwear fabrics. Guaranteed to spice up any evening.

Eye popping: Embroidered underwear. (Photographed in Wangfujing area)

Shoes

Looking to make a statement? If so, you could really get creative with embroidered shoes. You might even start a new fashion trend back home. Carp and lotus shoes anyone? Perhaps a kylin is more to your taste?

Feet come first: Plum blossom and bird pattern. (Photographed in Nanluogu Xiang)

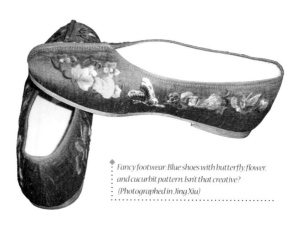

◆ *Fancy footwear: Blue shoes with butterfly, flower, and cucurbit pattern. Isn't that creative? (Photographed in Jing Xiu)*

Wall Hanging

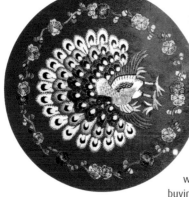

◆ *Feathered friend: A peacock-patterned wall hanging.*

Single-sided embroidery is suitable for getting framed and hanging on your wall. The right piece can become a superb addition to home decor. Pay attention to the background colors in the piece and make sure they suit the paint on your walls at home. If you are buying a gift for a friend, think about where they would most likely place it.

A distinguished dragon: As a protective creature, the dragon could be suitable for a front hallway.

Desk Decoration

These pieces, double-sided embroidery, are perfect for desks or tabletops. When you are looking for a suitable piece for your desk or for your dining table, there are many appropriate themes to choose from. Do you want to be a smart scholar or a consummate chef?

Crystal desk decoration: inside is a peach blossom and butterfly pattern. (Photographed in White Peacock Art World)

◆ *Flower Power: Embroidered peony and lotus. (Photographed in White Peacock Art World)*

◆ *Fantastic, fishy folding screen: Fish represent surplus, and eight represents fortune. A great tabletop metaphor! (Photographed in White Peacock Art World)*

Collector's Treasures

There are many people out there — including many reading this book — who are interested in buying embroidery for investment purposes only. However, there are also people who search for hard-to-find works, and build collections based on their idiosyncratic tastes.

If you are one of these people, then handmade pieces are of real interest to you. Since machine-made pieces tend to be mass-produced, they are not unique and do not arouse the interest of a collector of unusual embroidery.

The following is a brief glance at a few of the special collections different people have amassed over the years.

Unique Shoes

How cute! Your feet are an important part of your body. If your feet are not aligned properly, the whole body can be affected. The Chinese have taken special care of their feet. Perhaps the most infamous is the practice of binding women's feet from a young age to ensure they remained very small.

Out of the ordinary: Miao-style, butterfly-pattern shoes. (Photographed in Wangfujing area)

Even if this practice was cruel, it underscores the importance of feet in Chinese culture. Perhaps that is why on a child's hundredth day of life they would give them a special pair of shoes such as these. These shoes are thought to both protect and bless their owner. Some of the designs are quite funky, and would be difficult to find in any Western city.

◆ *Antique delights: Old embroidered shoes for children. (Photographed in Pan Yuzhen's home)*

◆ *Triple the fun: Three pairs of embroidered shoes. (Photographed in Wangfujing area)*

Distinctive Dresses

According to current Western standards, traditional Chinese dress is anything but conservative. It is rare to see somebody walking down the street with an embroidered dragon on his silk shirt, for example.

However, that is normal in traditional Chinese clothing. If you want to get really freaky, you can find items a whole lot more unusual. This is especially true of stage clothing used in Beijing Opera. If you have seen Farewell My Concubine, you will remember Yu Ji, the man who is confused about his gender. His hobby is collecting beautiful stage costumes.

Crafty imitations: A replica of Qing-style embroidered dress. (Photographed in White Peacock Art World)

Opera who built a museum for stage dresses in Shanghai. An avid collector, he began to accumulate stage clothing even before the Cultural Revolution. He is so passionate about his collection that he never sells pieces, and looks upon the idea of buying merely for economic gain with disdain. To him each of his pieces is a priceless work of art. He is also a creative spirit, and has developed some unique designs himself.

The dress showed here is not an antique. It is a modern replica of a Qing Dynasty dress. If you are a little unsure about verifying antique work, a replica is another option you could take. Replicas are cheaper but still have the advantages of being handmade, as well as possessing an antique-style appearance. And if you maintain it well, the price will not drop with time. As less people are interested in taking up embroidery as a profession, these pieces are gradually becoming rarer.

At this point in time, Qing Dynasty costumes are considered the most beautiful and precious. If you would like to get a taste of what these gowns look like, visit the Forbidden City. As Empress Dowager Cixi was an avid Beijing Opera fan, there is a considerable collection of Qing dynasty dresses there.

In Shanghai, the most famous collection is owned by Bao Wanrong, another fan of Beijing

Exquisitely Petite

In the Qing Dynasty, life was hard. Peasant women from the countryside crowded Beijing in order to find menial jobs such as waiting. As they did not earn enough, they spent their spare time making small, embroidered items to sell and earn a little extra.

Chairman of the Beijing Ancient Embroidery Association, Wang Jinhua began to collect embroidery almost by accident in 1968, during the Cultural Revolution. At the time, life was extremely hard. Mr.Wang was living in a village in Shanxi province and working as a manual laborer. Sometimes he bought small, embroidered items from local farmers for less than 1 RMB each. Today some of them are worth thousands. He

◆ *Capital class: A Jing Xiu-style bird, butterfly, and flower-patterned bag. (Photographed in Jing Xiu)*

had chanced upon some antique Qing dynasty creations.

If you purchase one of these antique pieces, chances are it has a remarkable story to tell. Maybe a wife sent it to her husband before he went to war or a girl to her boy before he went to the big city to participate in the Imperial Exam.

You can also buy modern replicas of this kind of work at a fraction of the price. This picture is an imitation Jing Xiu-style bird, butterfly, and flower pattern.

Ethnic Embroidery

Instead of written records, some traditional cultures recorded their history through the oral tradition. Others recorded it through painted art. The Miao recorded theirs through embroidery.

The first two pictures are parts of a ceremonial costume known as Guzang. They belong to Miao embroidery legend Pan Yuzheng, who we introduced earlier and have connection to a traditional Miao legend.

Great Guzang: An ancient Miao ceremonial costume – back side.
(Photographed in Pan Yuzhen's home)

Timeless ritual: The ceremonial costume – front side. (Photographed in Pan Yuzhen's home)

◆ *Zodiac rat: A Han horoscope symbol. (Photographed in Pan Yuzhen's home) In the Chinese zodiac, a rat is thought to be forthright, disciplined, systematic, meticulous, and charismatic. However they can also be manipulative and cruel. If you were born in 1948, 1960, 1972, or 1984 you are probably a mouse.*

Far back in time, the Miao people were nomadic. They wandered thousands of miles in search of suitable places in which to settle a short while, until one day they chanced upon a place in the high mountains of Southeast Yunnan. The day they arrived there, their dogs went crazy; running, rolling, and barking far out into the distance. When they returned, they had grains stuck to their fur.

◆ *A sticky situation: Man and butterfly versus tiger. (Photographed in Pan Yuzhen's home) The butterfly is thought to be the totemic ancestor of the Miao people, and imbued with protective powers. So this situation—a man with babies facing a tiger is not as serious as it may seem, due to the fact the butterfly is watching over them.*

The chief saw this and thought it was a good sign for the fertility of the land, and so the tribe stopped and planted crops there. A few months later, at harvest time, the chief's foresight proved correct. It was a bumper harvest for that year, and the next

13 years, after which the people decided to settle permanently in this bountiful place.

To commemorate this special occasion, the tribe dressed in these Guzang clothes and held a celebratory ritual at which an ox was sacrificed.

You can see the style is markedly different from Han embroidery. Intriguingly, though, Han cultural traditions are meshed into the work as well. The picture with the rat, for example, depicts one of the 12 animals in the Chinese zodiac.

Piece Made by a Master

This masterpiece was created by the venerable Chen Shaofang, an expert in the less popular Guang Xiu style who has won dozens of prizes from 1960s onward for her incredible work. This particular piece depicts a crane ballet dancing.

Guang Xiu was once popular in Guangdong, but is quickly becoming rarer. To try and salvage the skill and preserve them for future generations, Chen Shaofang established

◆ *Too hot to handle: People on the Sun. Miao people embroidered their history as a way to aid their memories. (Photographed in Pan Yuzhen's home)*

◆ *Careening crane: Have you ever seen a bird ballet? (Provided by Chen Shaofang)*

a research center in 1993 with the help of her family. However, even she is not very hopeful of the survival of her art form, and at over 70 years of age, she doesn't have much time or energy left to train new generations of embroiderers.

The wonderful skill of Guang Xiu is slowly being lost, which means that prices are rapidly on the rise. If you want to invest in works made by real masters, Guang Xiu is a good choice of style. Once again, make sure you have what you really think you have, and get the master to sign their name on the piece if possible. That way you will know it's authentic and its value will rise quickly.

Shopping
Spots

Some Buying Practice

Finding niche stores in a foreign country can be difficult. Ever been at a complete loss as to where to buy what you want? Allow me to take you on a guided tour through some of my most well connected and favorite stores throughout the Middle Kingdom. The selection I have given you is over a wide geographical area and makes an attempt to cater to all styles, including some of the lesser-known genres. There is a slight bias toward Beijing, due to the fact that Beijing has more visitors, but other cities are also catered for.

Why only buy from recommend stores? Importantly, especially in China where copied goods can be found in abundance, these stores are personally guaranteed to carry genuine handmade embroidery. If you are looking for the authentic article, complete with certificates or quality assurance, you can be certain to find it at the following businesses.

Ready to shop? Of course you are! Here are some commonsense steps to acquiring better bargaining skills.

Sharpening Your Bargaining Skills

Who hasn't, on occasion, paid a ridiculous price for what looks like great clothing/art/electronics whatever? Unfortunately when it comes to haggling over price, it sometimes feels like the vendor is the hunter and you are the prey!

And China is one place where everything — and I mean that almost literally — can be haggled over. After a year of living in the country I went to buy a new

Full frontal: A view of an embroidery shop.
(Photographed in Gongmei Building of Wangfujing)

phone. There are all kinds of places to do this, but I had always assumed — wrongly as it turned out — that cell phones in stores that have marked prices cannot be bargained for. I'd just got over this epiphany when I decided to look at SIM cards. The one I wanted was 280 kuai.

"Oh, that's ok, it's too expensive," I said, not too concerned about waiting for another day.

"You can have it for 200," said the sales assistant.

Overall, I bought the phone and the SIM card together for 400 kuai less than what was marked, and I wasn't even trying!

Many Westerners dislike bargaining, however, it can be surprisingly enjoyable. A spirited discussion over price is not just acceptable, it's expected. If you spend enough time doing it, it is also a great way to interact with the local people. If you are offering a decent price and have a friendly demeanor, you may also be able to have many an interesting cross-

◆ *Hardened veteran: Laowais (foreigners) who live in China for a long time often spot*
⋮ *tourists paying far too much.*

cultural exchange in English and maybe even Chinese.

If you go into a situation prepared in the mind, you should be able to buy what you want at a price that is fair to the vendor and reasonable to you. It is not good to pay too much. Remember that the next tourist who ventures into the lion's den will then be subjected to some outrageous price. It's good to keep these pointers in mind:

- Be patient: If you want to go on a shopping spree, and who doesn't, remember buying in China is not necessarily as simple as just picking up items and taking them to the cashier. Don't allow the vendor to rush you, because they will often try to shock you into parting with hard earned cash before you realize exactly what you are doing. Check the quality thoroughly.

- Don't look incredibly eager: Yes, it may be the most amazing shirt you've ever seen and you can't wait to burn it up the dance floor back home, but a vendor will sense your willingness to buy quite like a shark can smell blood! Take a lesson from my experience with the phone. Sometimes it's even better to appear more interested in the shirt next to it!

- Get at least two prices: Trust me, this is crucial. Patiently haggle with the vendor, then tell them politely you are interested and may come back. Often they will drop the price further, but if they don't, go and find the same or similar piece elsewhere and repeat the process. You may be amazed at the difference in price you can get.

- Retreat is often the best form of attack: Especially in crowded market places, it seems like the average vendor would rather give it to you than let you buy from someone else. It's an act of course, they'll still make their money, but remember to play the game successfully you need to act too.

There are many vendors out there who will give you an opening price that is literally 10 times what the piece is worth, especially if they think you are soft.

Remember to stay firm, relaxed, and enjoy yourself. Happy hunting!

Details of Stores

Beijing

White Peacock Art World
白孔雀艺术世界
báikǒngquè yìshù shìjiè

 No.3 Dongbinhe St. Dewai
Beijing China (Subway
station: Gulou Dajie)
北京市西城区德胜门外东
滨河路3号

 010-62018084 62011199

 Ji Desheng, Liu Xin

 www.bkq.com.cn

The White Peacock is a place for the true connoisseur of art. You can find everything imaginable here: handmade, pure silk rugs, woolen carpets, art tapestries, paintings, carved lacquer ware, jade ware, wood, and stone carving ware...but most of the embroidery is exhibited and sold on the third floor. For the main part the works on offer are Su Xiu embroidery, but there are also good examples of Yue Xiu and others. You can find embroidered scarves, pajamas, and dresses here too. I would suggest setting aside at least half a day to visit this place, if not a whole day.

Goulswon
古吴绣皇
gǔwú xiùhuáng

 Shi Jingyan, Zhang Feng

 010-87795805-8004
13811880558 (Shi)
010-87795805-8006
13391 8546 (Zhang)

 artishen@163.com
www.goulswon.com

This is a famous and highly regarded name in the embroidery world, with 15 stores around the country. Goulswon emphasizes selling top-quality Su Xiu, which are suitable for both collection purposes and to appreciate in the home. The pictures speak for themselves.

The world of embroidery. Display area in White Peacock Art World. (Photographed in White Peacock Art World)

Age-old art: Embroidery of still life.
(Provided by Goulswon)

Goulswon in Shinkong Place Center
古美绣皇新光天地店

✉ 5th Floor, No.18 Building, No. 89 of Jianguo Road, Chaoyang District, Beijing
北京市朝阳区建国路89号18号楼5层

☎ 010-65981744

Goulswon in China World Shopping Mall
古美绣皇国贸店

✉ No. WB119, B1 Floor, China World Shopping Mall, No. 1 of Jianguomen Wai Street, Beijing
北京市建国门外大街1号国贸商城B1/WB119号

☎ 010-65056226

Goulswon in Main Store of Yansha
古美绣皇燕莎店

✉ 5th Floor, No.52 of Liangmaqiao Road, Chaoyang District, Beijing
北京市朝阳区亮马桥路52号5层

☎ 010-65651188-540

Twilight pastime: A girl dancing in moonlight.
(Provided by Goulswon)

Goulswon in Zhongguancun Area

古美绣皇中关村店

✉ No. B9-11, Business Walking Street of Zhongguancun Plaza, Haidian District, Beijing
北京市海淀区中关村广场
商业步行街B9／B10／B11号

☎ 010-51721651

Goulswon in Golden Resource New Yansha Mall

古美绣皇金源店

✉ Ground Floor of Guiyou Building, No.1 Yuanda Road , Haidian District, Beijing
北京市海淀区远大路1号
金源购物中心贵友大厦1层

☎ 010-88875073

Goulswon in SCITECH

古美绣皇赛特店

✉ Underground 2nd Floor, No22 Jianguomen Wai Street
建国门外大街22号地下2层

☎ 010-65124488-6709

Gorgeous gown: An embroidered dress sold by Madame Pan. (Photographed in Pan Yuzhen's home)

Zitange Su Xiu Embroidery Shop

紫樘间苏绣精品组

zǐtángé sūxiù jīngpǐnzǔ

✉ 3rd Floor, Gongmei Building, No.200 of Wangfujing Street (Subway station: Wangfujing)
北京市王府井大街200号
工美大厦3层

☎ 010-65251819

👤 Liu Shuling

Hidden corner: Zitange Su Xiu Embroidery Store.(Photographed in Gongmei Building)

Don't be misled by the name. Xiang Xiu can also be found here. Besides your traditional wall-hanging type embroidery, you can also find embroidered cards, handkerchiefs, and small decorations as souvenirs. Located at Wangfujing, this is very accessible even if you are only in Beijing for a day or two. It's also a sentimental favorite of mine because it was the first place I saw embroidery in China.

Guanzhe

观者

guānzhě

 No.18, Underground 1st Floor, Beijing Building Materials Trade Tower, Dongtucheng Road, Beijing
北京市朝阳区东土城路
北京建材经贸大厦
地下1层18号

 010-85271053
13621081367

 Zhang Xin

The visual feast on offer at Guanzhe includes embroidered scenery, human figures, animals, and flowers. Even more intriguing, they can embroider according to your personal needs. Would you like to have an embroidered picture of yourself or one of your pet?

Jing Xiu

京绣

jīngxiù

 No. 1 of Fuxiang Hutong, Nanluogu Xiang, Ping'an Street, Beijing
北京市平安大街南锣鼓巷
福祥胡同1号

 13911119600

 Jin Xin

The owner of Jing Xiu, Ms Jin Xin, designs the products of this store herself in an effort to differentiate her business from others and

Top-notch two: Wallets designed by Jin Xin. (Photographed in Jing Xiu)

maintain a creatively unique style. All the pieces available here are Jing Xiu style — fit for an emperor. On display you can see elaborate handmade wallet, business card box, shoes, small bags, and dresses. The shop itself is located in a delightful, old Beijing neighborhood that is now famous for its bars. When you come by for a drink, why not pop into Jing Xiu?

Miao Xiu Stand in Panjiayuan Collection Market

贵州台江民族民间服饰
织锦工艺厂驻京办事处

pānjiāyuán miáoxiù tān

 No.3-4, Row 21, No.3 District, Panjiayuan Collection Market, Beijing
北京市潘家园旧货市场3区
21排3-4号摊

 010-87720338
13051566202

 Pan Yuzhen

Madame Pan, proprietor of the Miao Xiu stand is almost a legendary figure, as many of her pieces have been collected by museums and she has participated in exhibitions in several countries. The stand sells antique dresses, handmade silver objects, wall hangings, bags, shoes, and hats, all loaded with cultural significance. If you would like to have something tailor-made for yourself it is possible, although it will definitely take some time.

Lamu

楼上的拉姆

lóushàng de lāmǔ

◆ *Clothing or decoration: Colorful embroidered dress hanging on a peach-flower-painted wall. (Photographed in Lamu)*

✉ No.117, Nanluogu Xiang, Dongcheng District, Beijing
北京市东城区南锣鼓巷117号

📞 010-64035609

👤 Zhang Shulin, Liu Jun

e www.lamucn.com

Everything for sale at Lamu is a unique original! You can find dresses, bags, cushions, and more. The majority of the work is Miao Xiu, and flowers and vivid colors are in plentiful supply.

Emperor

皇锦

huángjǐn

If you want to feel like an emperor in your own home, then Emperor will meet your tastes. The embroidery here is both elegantly oriental and sumptuously royal, characterized by soft colors and exquisite techniques.

◆ *Imperial comfort: An embroidered cushion. (Provided by Emperor)*

Emperor in China World Shopping Mall
皇锦国贸商城店

 No.NB119, China World
Shopping Mall, No. 1 of
Jianguomen Wai Street,
Beijing
北京市建国门外大街1号
中国国际贸易中心商场
NB148

☎ 010-65056146

👤 Qiu Ying (Amanda)

Emperor in Oriental Plaza
皇锦东方广场店

✉ No. AA12, Oriental Plaza,
No. 1 of East Chang'an
Street, Beijing
北京东长安街1号
东方广场AA12

☎ 010-8518 6148

👤 Xie Zhongying (Maria)

Shanghai

Shuoyong Fangjian
硕勇坊间工作室
shuòyǒng fǎngjiān gōngzuòshì

✉ Room 118, No. 3, Lane 210,
Art Street,Taikang Road,
Luwan District, Shanghai
上海市卢湾区泰康路艺术
街210弄3号118室

☎ 021-64734566
13301872276

👤 Zhang Yan

If you are super keen on
embroidery, Shuoyong Fangjian
has got something very
special for you; it will teach
you how to embroider!
They do, of course, also sell
embroidery.

Emperor
皇锦
huángjǐn

✉ No. 201, No.1376 of West
Nanjing Road, Shanghai
Center
上海南京西路1376号上海
商城201号

☎ 021-62798711

👤 Chen Bing (Iccey)
Li Li (Lily)

Suzhou

Mingying Embroidery
明莹刺绣美术工作室
míngyíng cìxiù měishù
gōngzuòshì

✉ No.9 of Jing Xiang,
Guanqian Street, Suzhou
苏州市观前街井巷9号

☎ 0512-67279207

👤 Zhou Yinghua

🅔 www.my-embroidery.com

Mingying is known for its
particular affinity for embroidery
based on paintings, both

Chinese and Western. They also create excellent photograph-based work. Their works include decorative or daily-use items, and souvenirs or gifts. You can find single-sided, double-sided, and hair embroidery here.

Goulswon

古吴绣皇

gǔwú xiùhuáng

✉ No. 314 of Xiupin Street, Zhenhu of High-tech District, Suzhou
苏州市高新区镇湖绣品街314号

✆ 0512-66912585

👤 Shi Jingyan
(010-87795805-8004
13811880558)
Zhang Feng
(010-87795805-8006
13391 8546)

Tengqun Xiuzhuang

腾群绣庄

téngqún xiùzhuāng

✉ No 318 of Xiupin Street, High-tech District, Suzhou
苏州高新区绣品街318号

✆ 0512-61916500

👤 Liu Junjun

Tengqun features handmade single- and double-sided Su Xiu. You can ask them to embroider according to your special needs, including portraits of people.

◆ *Proud and provocative: A peacock.*
(Provided by Goulswon)

Changsha

Zaihong Xiang Xiu Embroidery

再红湘绣

zaìhóng xiāngxiù

🄴 www.zaihong.com.cn

Zaihong is a lady who was born into a seventh-generation family of embroiderers. A master of needlework, she has won numerous prizes and her name has subsequently become a brand of Xiang Xiu embroidery. You can find four of these stores around Changsha, the capital of Hunan province.

Zaihong Xiang Xiu in
再红湖绣友谊商城店

✉ 1st Floor of Friendship Shopping Center, Dongtang District, Changsha
长沙市东塘友谊商城1层

☎ 13875884097

👤 Shen Libing

Zaihong Xiang Xiu in
再红湖绣友谊商店店

✉ 6th Floor, B Hall, Friendship Store, Yuangjialing, Changsha
长沙市袁家岭友谊商店B馆6层

☎ 13787182784

👤 Liu Hongbo

Zaihong Xiang Xiu in
再红湖绣阿波罗商业广场店

✉ 3rd Floor, Apollo Business Plaza, North Chezhan Road, Changsha
长沙市车站北路阿波罗商业广场3层

☎ 13973186580

👤 Wu Shuo

Zaihong Xiang Xiu in
再红湖绣家润多店

✉ Joindoor Hypermarket, Renmin Road, Changsha
长沙市人民路立交桥西家润多百货店内

☎ 13974928132

👤 Jiang Qing

Sales Department of Hunan Xiang Xiu Embroidery Museum
湖南湘绣博物馆刺绣经营都
húnán xiāngxiù bówùguǎn cìxiù jīngyíngbù

✉ No. 39 of North Chezhan Road, Changsha
湖南省长沙市车站北路39号

☎ 0731-2291820

👤 Shen Zong

This is a great place to buy Xiang Xiu no matter what your budget, as prices range from very low to very high. Even better, it is conveniently located on the way to the Xiang Xiu Embroidery Museum.

Guangzhou

Best Guang Xiu Embroidery
广绣精品
guǎngxiù jīngpǐn

✉ No. 289 of South Kangwang Road, Liwan District, Guangzhou (Inside Jinlun Huiguan)
广东省广州市荔湾区康王南路289号（锦纶会馆内）

☎ 13928815909

👤 Li Min

This is predominantly a showcase of the best of Guang Xiu, which is a style of Yue Xiu. Many of the pieces here are made by master Chen Shaofang, but only a few are for sale. However for a visual feast of Guang Xiu, it's the place to see.

Sales Department of Guang Xiu Research Institute

广绣研究所销售部

guǎngxiù yánjiūsuǒ xiāoshòubù

✉ No. 289 of South Kangwang Road, Liwan District, Guangzhou (Inside Jinlun Huiguan)
广东省广州市荔湾区康王南路289号 （锦纶会馆内）

☎ 020-35687844 81956079
13250258259

👤 Yang Feng

The Sales Dep also sell Guang Xiu embroidery. This could be a good future investment, because as a relatively obscure art form, the numbers of experts are rapidly diminishing. Guang Xiu is now already becoming quite rare.

◆ *More detail: A closer view of the flower and the bird.*

Chengdu

Jinxiuma

锦绣玛

jǐn xiù mǎ

✉ No 18, Xinghui Road, Chengdu
成都市星辉路18号

☎ 13980801217

👤 Ma Tisheng

ℯ www.shujin.net

Jinxiuma specialize in beautiful, handmade Shu Xiu. You can also enjoy the famous Shu brocade here.

◆ *Two is company: A bird and a butterfly meet and chat happily. (Provided by Chen Shaofang)*

Appendix

Chinese Phrases Used in Buying Embroidery

● ***This is very pretty.***

zhè gè hěn piào liàng
这   个   很   漂 亮。

● ***Can I take a look?***

wǒ kě yǐ kàn kàn ma
我   可   以   看   看   吗?

● ***Can I try it on?***

wǒ kě yǐ shì yi xià ma
我   可   以   试   一   下   吗?

● ***I like this one.***

wǒ xǐ huān zhè ge
我   喜   欢   这   个。

● ***I don't like this one.***

wǒ bù xǐ huān zhè ge
我   不   喜   欢   这   个。

● ***Do you have a different color?***

nǐ yǒu bié de
你   有   别   的

yán sè ma
颜   色   吗?

● ***Too small.***

tài xiǎo
太   小。

● ***Too big.***

tài dà
太   大。

◆ *Pyjama party. Buying embroidered night wear.*

Do you have_____(insert color)?

nǐ   yǒu _____(insert color) de   ma
你   有 _____(insert color)   的   吗?

How to say colors in Chinese.

Colors	Chinese pinyin	Chinese characters
green	lǜ sè	绿色
black	hēi sè	黑色
pink	fěn sè	粉色
gray	huī sè	灰色
yellow	huáng sè	黄色
blue	lán sè	蓝色
white	bái sè	白色
red	hóng sè	红色

I want to buy_____(insert name).

wǒ   xiǎng mǎi _____ (insert name)
我   想   买_____ (insert name).

How to say the names of the different Chinese embroidery styles.

Names	Chinese pinyin	Chinese characters
Su Xiu Embroidery	sū xiù	苏绣
Xiang Xiu Embroidery	xiāng xiù	湘绣
Shu Xiu Embroidery	shǔ xiù	蜀绣
Yue Xiu Embroidery	yuè xiù	粤绣
Miao Xiu Embroidery	miáo xiù	苗绣
Jing Xiu Embroidery	jīng xiù	京绣
Double-sided Embroidery	shuāng miàn xiù	双面绣

Is this handmade?

zhè   shì   shǒu gōng   de   ma
这   是   手   工   的   吗?

Does it have a certificate?

yǒu zhèng shū   ma
有   证   书   吗?

What's the meaning of this pattern?

tú   àn   shì shén me   yì   si
图   案   是   什   么   意   思?

Which kind of wood is this frame made from?

kuāng zi   shì   shén me   mù   tou
框   子   是   什   么   木   头?

I want to buy this one.

wǒ   yào   mǎi   zhè   ge
我   要   买   这   个。

How much is this?

duō   shǎo qián
多   少   钱?

I want to buy that one.

wǒ   yào   mǎi
我   要   买

nà   ge
那   个。

Too expensive! (Believe me, you're going to use this one a lot.)

tài   guì   le
太   贵   了!

Stay firm: Practicing bargaining skills.

Can you give it to me a little cheaper? (And this one.....)

gěi wǒ pián yi yī diǎn er
给 我 便 宜 一 点 儿?

Please give me the lowest price!

wǒ yào zuì dī jià
我 要 最 低 价!

I didn't bring that much cash with me.

wǒ qián bú gòu
我 钱 不 够。

Can I pay by_____ (insert the method of payment)?

kě yǐ yòng _____(insert the way of payment) ma
可 以 用 _____(insert the way of payment) 吗?

How to say the methods of payment in Chinese

Names	Chinese pinyin	Chinese characters
U.S. dollar	měi yuán	美元
Euro	ōu yuán	欧元
Pound	yīng bàng	英镑
Credit card	xìn yòng kǎ	信用卡
Traveler's check	lǚ xíng zhī piào	旅行支票

Can you write me a tax receipt?

kě yǐ tuì shuì ma
可 以 退 税 吗?

Please give me change.

qǐng zhǎo wǒ líng qián
请 找 我 零 钱.

Please wrap it for me.

qǐng gěi wǒ bāo zhuāng
请 给 我 包 装。

I don't want the frame.

wǒ bú yào kuāng zi
我 不 要 框 子。

Wrap the embroidery and the frame separately.

xiù、 kuāng fēn kāi bāo zhuāng
绣、 框 分 开 包 装。

Can you explain how to install the embroidery in the frame?

qǐng jiāo wǒ ān zhuāng
请 教 我 安 装。

I only want to buy this one.

wǒ zhǐ mǎi zhè yí gè
我 只 买 这 一 个。

Thank you, good-bye!

xiè xiè
谢 谢,

zài jiàn
再 见!

◆ Be sure: Do you need any extras?

Watch Your Tone

Most of the difficulties in speaking and understanding Mandarin as a second language are credited to mastering its four tones. These four tones can give the same sound for four entirely different meanings. What we forget is that the implication of a word in English can change quite a bit by using the very same four tones. Let us take, by way of example, the frequently used semi-adverb "yeah."

First Tone

Use the same tone as you would for a resigned, drawn out "yeah."
Coworker: "The boss asked you to work this weekend too, huh?"
You: "Yeah..."

Second Tone

Use the tone reserved for the rising, questioning, almost hesitant "yeah."
Spouse: "We have a big problem we need to discuss."
You: "Yeah?"

Third Tone

This one calls for a dip followed by a rise in tone, a tone of pride or confirmation. You can't go wrong if you dip the chin and raise it again when using it.
Friend: "You told the taxi driver how to get there, in Chinese?"
You: "Yeah-uh."

Fourth Tone

This is the quick, sharp tone of emphasis, the one used for leaving no doubt.
Babysitter: "I'm supposed to make sure he doesn't play on the roof, right?"
You: "Yeah!"

Neutral Tone

As for the neutral tone, it isn't nearly as mysterious as it might sound. It is pronounced quickly, as an afterthought or cushion between words, much as a quick English "um" or "uh." It occurs in two important particles – the "ma" used to make a statement a question, and "de," used to make a noun an adjective or possessive. In terms of "yeah," it would equate to "Yeah look, we've heard enough about tones and are ready to start practicing."

Thanks

Yueyuan Ren thanks: Spring Su, my best friend and photographer of this book, who shows you the amazing beauty of Chinese embroidery art; Liwei Zhang and Daisy Jing who did the fun illustrations in the book; Pan Yuzhen, an expert in Miao Xiu, who told us the stories behind each art piece; Chen Shaofang, a renowned master, who provided us with photos of gorgeous Guang Xiu embroidery art.

Thanks also go to the White Peacock Art World, Goulswon, Jing Xiu and other shops whose kind assistance has enabled us to provide our readers with the beautiful photographs.

My special thanks go to Rhys Wesley, the main author of the book, for his devotion to perfect the book.

Last but not the least, a big THANK YOU to all who have rendered help in presenting this nice little book to the world.

The publishers would like to thank you, our dear readers, for purchasing the book! To improve the title and make it a real handy and up-to-date manual is our ultimate goal. We thus ask your kind feedback to the book by dropping a note to us at the following email address: MCBeijing@gmail.com. We will pass your feedback to the authors. We may incorporate your comments/suggestions to the next edition. If you don't want us to do so or to have your name acknowledged, please kindly indicate. We will present you with a complimentary copy of the next edition if your comments/suggestions contribute notably to the improvement of the title.